HISTORY OF
WESTERN
MOVIES

Happy Birthday Papa Lute
This is nothing serious---
Just For Fun.
Much Love.
Marietta + David

4/7/85

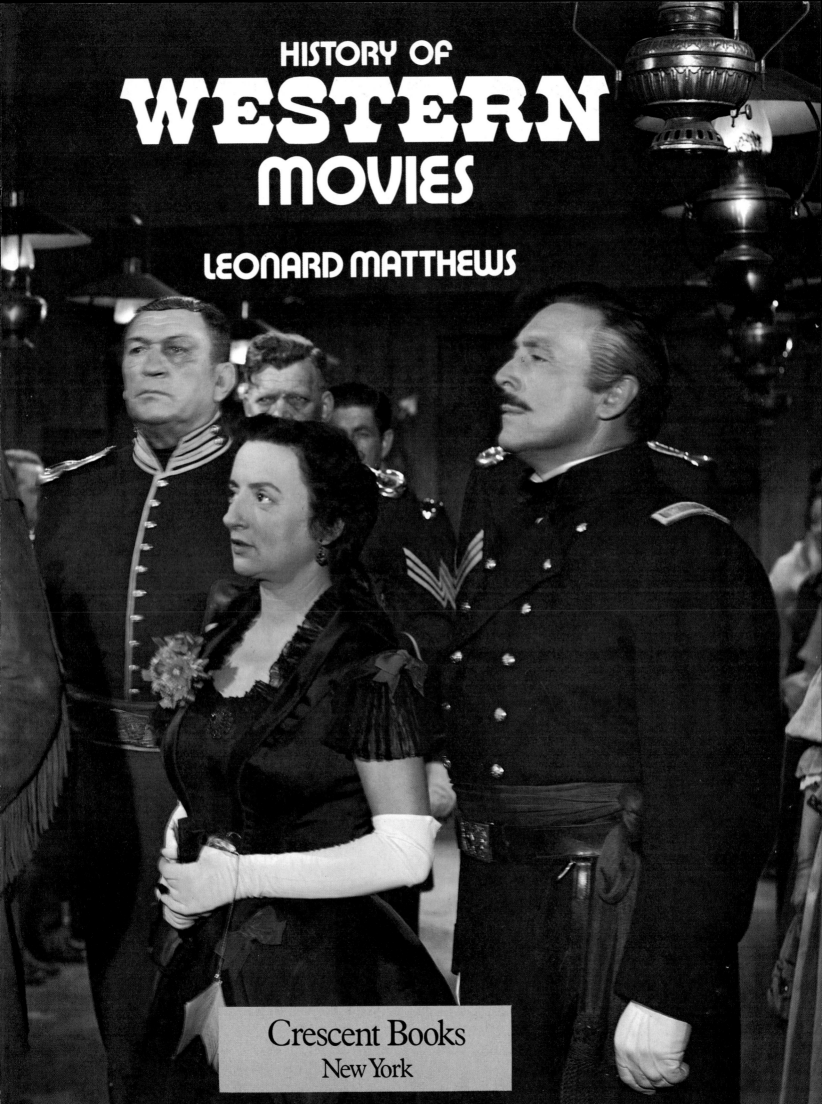

HISTORY OF
WESTERN
MOVIES

LEONARD MATTHEWS

Crescent Books

New York

Picture acknowledgments
© Walt Disney Productions, page 136; Flashbacks, London,
pages 135, 143, 168, 171; Kobal Collection, London, pages 7,
9, 10 top, 11, 14, 15, 16, 19, 21, 22, 24, 25, 28–29, 31, 32, 33, 34,
35, 36, 37, 39, 40, 41, 42 bottom, 43, 44, 46, 51, 53, 54, 58, 60,
62, 63, 74, 75, 76, 77 bottom, 78, 79, 80, 81, 85, 87 bottom, 89
bottom, 91, 97, 99, 100, 104, 108, 110, 120, 122, 123 bottom,
124, 125, 126 top, 127, 129, 133, 134, 137 top, 138, 139, 140,
141, 142, 144, 145, 146, 148, 150 top, 152, 153 top, 155, 157,
159, 160, 161, 163, 166, 169, 172, 175, 176, 178, 180, 181, 182,
183, 184, 185, 187; Martspress Ltd., Surrey, pages 8 bottom,
10 bottom, 12, 13, 17, 18, 20, 23, 26, 27, 38, 45, 47, 48, 49, 52,
55, 56, 57, 59, 61, 64, 65, 67, 68, 69, 70, 71, 72, 73, 77 top, 82,
83, 84, 86, 87 top, 88, 89 top, 90, 92, 94, 95, 96, 98, 101, 102,
103, 107, 109, 111, 112, 113, 114–115, 116, 117, 118, 119, 121,
123 top, 126 bottom, 128, 130, 131, 132, 137 bottom, 149, 150
bottom, 151, 153 bottom, 154, 156, 158, 162, 164, 165, 167,
170, 173, 174, 177, 179, 186; National Film Archive, London,
pages 8 top, 42 top, 50, 66, 93

Front cover: *The Magnificent Seven* (Kobal Collection)
Back cover: *The Alamo* (Kobal Collection)
Endpapers: *The Covered Wagon* (Kobal Collection)
Title page: *She Wore a Yellow Ribbon* (Kobal Collection)

First English edition published by
Deans International Publishing
52–54 Southwark Street, London SE1 1UA
A division of The Hamlyn Publishing Group Limited
London · New York · Sydney · Toronto

ISBN 0-517-414759

This 1984 edition is published by Crescent Books
Distributed by Crown Publishers, Inc.
h g f e d c b a

Printed in Italy

Contents

The Trail Blazers

Opposite: Max Aaronson alias Gilbert M. Anderson known to filmic fame as Broncho Billy. No real cowboy of the ranges would have worn such fancy duds, but how were cinema audiences all over the world to know that? He was adulated by millions.

The Great Train Robbery (1903), produced by the Edison Company, was not, as many people suppose, the first Western film. That accolade probably belongs to *Cripple Creek Bar-room* which the same studio had turned out in 1898.

After that, Edison filmed *The Life of an American Cowboy* (1902) and the following year *Western Stagecoach Hold-Up*. Both were directed by a movie-camera technician named Edwin Stanton Porter.

There were no story values as such in any of these films. They were single situations simply presented with little pretension to acting on the part of the performers.

The Great Train Robbery (1903) was also directed by Porter from a script consisting solely of a few notes he had jotted down on a pad. It was a script with a difference, though, for it outlined a definite story. Although only a few minutes in length, it was the first *story* Western and the next seventeen years were to see the extension of the Western from one-reel to six-reel action-packed movies starring some of the most famous film cowboys, Broncho Billy Anderson, William S. Hart, Tom Mix and Harry Carey.

The Godfather: Broncho Billy Anderson

At twenty-one, Gilbert Anderson, born Max Aaronson in Little Rock, Arkansas, in 1882, was working spasmodically as a photographer's model, a rather odd choice of livelihood for a young man with a big nose, a craggy jaw and jug ears.

Prior to this he had been a travelling salesman and then a vaudeville performer, when he had changed his name to Gilbert M. Anderson.

Always on the look-out for new opportunities, he was reading a newspaper one day when his eyes fell on the words 'Models required to pose before a camera. Apply Edison Studio, 23rd Street, Manhattan.' In a spirit of nothing ventured, nothing won he left his shabby room and headed for 23rd Street, Manhattan. Here he met thirty-two-year-old Edwin Stanton Porter. Born in Connellsville, Pennsylvania, a chequered career lay behind Porter. He had been a sign-painter, a plumber, a telegrapher, a tailor, a bill-poster, a stagehand, for three years a regular sailor in the US Navy, and then a mechanic for Raff and Gammon, a company which was distributing the Edison Vitascope. Later, he was associated with the famous inventor, Thomas A. Edison.

Unlike Edison, Porter was convinced that there was a big future for the movie camera and right now he was about to embark on a new film to be entitled *The Great Train Robbery*, a theme doubtless inspired by the nefarious activities of such Wild West bandits as Jesse and Frank James, the Younger Brothers, Butch Cassidy and the Sundance Kid.

Porter hired Gilbert Anderson because he looked right and he could, he said, ride a horse.

So began the film career of the first big-name Western film star, an actor whose impact on sagebrush films still runs like an unbreakable thread through today's Western films and television series, for Max Aaronson, alias Gilbert M. Anderson, is remembered today as 'Broncho Billy' Anderson,

On the first day of shooting *The Great*

Above: Emulating the dubious exploits of bandits such as Jesse James and Butch Cassidy, two no-goods display their metal in The Great Train Robbery *(Edison Company).*

Below: The hold-up in the telegraph office, the opening scene in The Great Train Robbery *(Edison Company).*

Train Robbery in New Jersey, Gilbert mounted the horse that had been singled out for him on the wrong side, hit the saddle and fell off. Although he fell off several more times, Porter did not fire him on the spot. He had been on the look-out for a volunteer who could fall off a horse without seriously hurting himself and Anderson had just done that.

Gilbert M. Anderson took it from there and by the time the film was completed, he had decided, despite his many bruises, that he would henceforth dedicate his life to the world of movies.

The Great Train Robbery, which ran for approximately ten minutes only, was a little masterpiece. Porter wrote the script and directed the whole action. Building from the opening shots of a train seen through a railroad depot window and the subduing of a telegraph operator by an armed gang of outlaws, the film progressed swiftly to its rousing climax of the pursuit and round-up of the badmen. Unusual for a silent film, it had no subtitles.

Never again was Porter to show the genius that he poured into *The Great Train Robbery*, probably because he was more fascinated by the technical aspects and development of the movie camera than by producing and directing.

If Porter was no longer willing to involve himself in the art of making movies, Gilbert M. Anderson surely was. At this time, he was not particularly interested in acting. He wanted to be a director rather than an actor and managed to get a job with the Vitagraph Corporation where he bent all his energies for the next two years to learning all he could about film-making.

He never forgot the success of *The Great Train Robbery* and yearned to make more Westerns, which was why he took off for Chicago to join the outfit of an ebullient movie producer, Colonel George Selig. In fact, Selig was not an army man, nor was he a Colonel. He had appropriated this title, perhaps to impress

SENSATIONAL AND STARTLING "HOLD UP" OF THE "GOLD EXPRESS" BY FAMOUS WESTERN OUTLAWS

the other 'ranks' serving with him in his company.

Though not very interested in filming Westerns, Selig all the same had a crew at work in Golden, not far from Denver, Colorado. Gilbert persuaded the Colonel to post him to the crew. Away he went, virtually took over the unit, rounded up a few cowboys and proceeded to rattle off some short Westerns.

Then the Colonel lost all interest in filming anything one mile further west than Lakeshore Drive, Chicago. Disenchanted with Selig's sudden lack of support, Anderson sped back to Chicago and sought out a friend, George K. Spoor.

Together they formed a company called Essanay, this being a linking of their initials. It was to acquire fame as the company which produced a series of sidesplitting slapstick shorts featuring the antics of a certain splay-footed English comedian wearing a seedy hard hat and baggy pants: Charles Spencer Chaplin.

Above: The film that started it all, The Great Train Robbery, *made by the Edison Studio in 1903.*

Below: Three famous film stars of the Essanay Studio circa 1915. Left, Francis X. Bushman; centre, the immortal Charlie Chaplin, and right, Broncho Billy Anderson.

Above: A hostile reception for Broncho Billy in The Settler's Daughter *(Essanay Studios.*

Below: A typical scene from a Broncho Billy movie that would have entranced cinemagoers.

Kyne and concerned the adventures of a cowboy hero called Broncho Billy.

With relish Anderson set to work to film the story but almost at once came up against a stumbling block. Who was to play Broncho Billy? There was nobody to hand suitable for the part, so Anderson decided to be Broncho Billy himself. He donned sombrero, woolly chaps, check shirt and loose neckerchief, threw a gun-belt round his waist and lo! the first of the great Wild West film characters was born. He revelled in the part. What he lacked in looks, he made up for in his rugged portrayal of a true-to-life Westerner.

There is some doubt as to which Broncho Billy film was made first but it was certainly a roaring success, the first of hundreds of Westerns produced by Essanay during the next five years, many of them featuring Broncho Billy Anderson. During their making, Anderson established every facet of the Western film as we know it today and created every character from badman hero and mysterious gunman-with-a-mission to unjustly ac-

Late in 1908 Anderson and his little crew were in Niles, near San Francisco. To cut their eye-teeth they had made a few short comedies in Los Angeles but now Gilbert was determined to start making Westerns again.

By chance he came across a short story in *The Saturday Evening Post*. It had been written by the well-known author Peter B.

cused young cowpoke and incorruptible sheriff as well as every set-up from range feuds to hell-fire bank raids.

By 1918, Anderson and Spoor had been arguing too long about whether they should continue with their short films while a dour ex-Shakespearean actor named William Surrey Hart and a one-time rodeo star named Tom Mix were appearing in feature-length Westerns which were capturing the public's imagination.

Too late, Essanay commenced *The Son of a Gun* (1918), a feature film in which Anderson played a down-and-out roustabout, an inglorious figure after the heroic Broncho Billy.

His great days were over. In the 1920s he turned his hand to producing some excellent Stan Laurel comedies, but Broncho Billy was a ghost of the past, never to ride again in another film.

Anderson drifted out of film-making and passed his last years at the Motion Picture Country House in Woodland Hills, dying in 1971.

'The Thrill of it All!': William S. Hart

If Broncho Billy was no Adonis, neither was William S. Hart. His tall bony figure was topped by a hatchet face illuminated by tiny flashing eyes and gashed by a rat-trap of a mouth.

Even so, it was a striking countenance that served him well during his years upon the legitimate stage. There he was so highly regarded that it was bandied around that his initial 'S' stood for Shakespeare. Actually, his middle name was Surrey.

He was born on 6 November 1870 in Newburgh, New York, the son of an itinerant miller who vagabonded his way across country, avowedly searching for new water sites. Coming to the Dakota

Bill Hart was still toiling away for Thomas Ince when he starred in The Square Deal Man *in 1917 (Ince-Triangle).*

WILLIAM S. HART in The SQUARE DEAL MAN

Territory, then Indian country, the family settled near a Sioux Indian reservation where the lad met the tribesmen and came to admire their way of life and culture.

When Bill Hart was in his teens, the family returned to New York where he took a job as postal clerk in the main post office. He was twenty when he was bitten by the acting bug and started to study acting seriously in his spare time. His efforts were rewarded with some success.

He first appeared as a professional actor in *Romeo and Juliet* and was still acting on stage in 1905 when he was sharing a room in a Broadway hotel with another actor and an eleven-year-old boy named Thomas Ince.

Years later, Hart was on tour in Cleveland, Ohio, when he happened to drop in at a cinema. He was unimpressed with the film that was being shown. It was purportedly a Western but his childhood days in Dakota informed him that the movie he was watching was inaccurate in the extreme, the people responsible for it obviously knowing no more about the true West than they did about the sex life of the tsetse fly.

The opportunity to make a *true* Wes-

tern came to him in autumn, 1912. Touring on stage in *The Trail of the Lonesome Pine*, he reached Los Angeles where he learned that a Western film in production was being directed by his one-time stable companion, Tom Ince.

Bill Hart went to the studio and let it be known that he was more than willing to help Ince produce better Westerns.

By the time Bill Hart renewed his acquaintance with Tom Ince in Los Angeles, Ince had become a fully fledged film director. He had hired the famous Wild West Show known as the Miller Brothers 101 Ranch to use in the making of his Western film, *War on the Plains* (1912).

The 101 Ranch's headquarters in Oklahoma was a vast stretch of Indian territory where a huge rodeo arena had been erected for the edification and entertainment of thousands of cheering tourists. Cowboys, cowgirls, Indians, hundreds of mustangs, oxen, longhorns and bison, as well as scores of prairie schooners and stage-coaches were all part of the show, which was why *War on the Plains* was the first *big* Western.

It was a *tour de force* for Tom Ince and he may well have felt proud of his achieve-

Opposite: William S. Hart's cinematic expressions ranged from A to B, from mobile to wooden, but here he is showing that on the odd occasion he could laugh.

Below: Unimpressed with Hart's efforts to bring reality to the Western, Tom Ince sold The Bargain *in 1914 to Famous Players. Ince was dead wrong for the movie was an immediate success (Thomas H. Ince).*

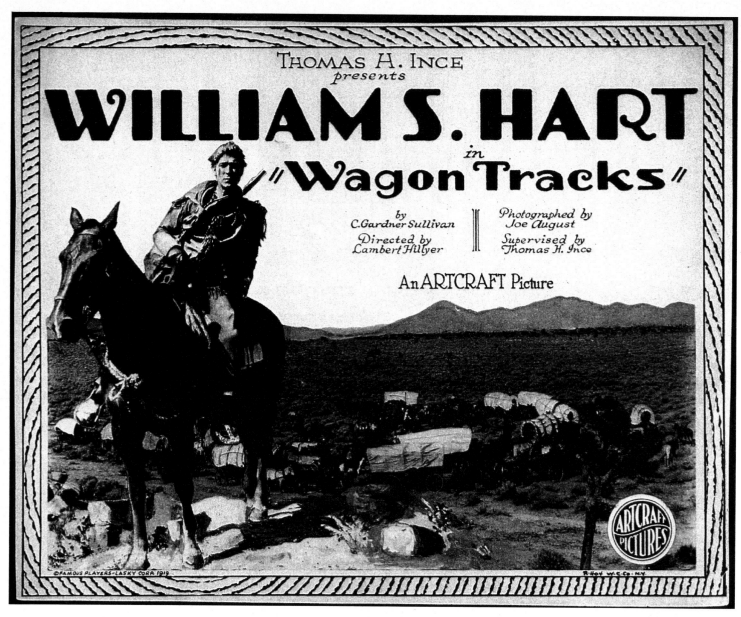

THOMAS H. INCE
presents

WILLIAM S. HART

in
"Wagon Tracks"

by
C. Gardner Sullivan

Photographed by
Joe August

Directed by
Lambert Hillyer

Supervised by
Thomas H. Ince

An ARTCRAFT Picture

©FAMOUS PLAYERS-LASKY CORP 1919

ment as he sat listening to Bill Hart telling him how Westerns should be made.

As it so happened, Westerns were suffering a temporary lapse in their popularity, and it was not for another year that Hart won a contract from Ince, for 75 dollars a week. He started off by expanding a two-reeler script from Ince into a feature-length film.

Ince read it, liked it and decided to produce it. He even allowed Hart to play the part he had written into the script with himself in mind. This was Texas, an outlaw who, for love of a fair lady, allowed himself to be reformed by the town preacher. It was the sort of type-casting in which Hart was to revel for years, even to the ending when the reverend gentleman blissfully kisses the girl while Bill unhygienically kisses his horse.

When the film, *On the Night Stage* (1915), was completed, Ince was not so impressed but, anxious to keep Bill busy,

he found a new part for the gaunt actor in another Western, *The Bargain* (1914), a five-reeler.

Bill poured more of his notions into the film but when it was finished, Tom Ince was still doubtful and lost heart at the prospect of making yet another Western. Lost heart and lost Hart, for when he told Bill, the actor decided to head back to Broadway and the legitimate stage.

Meanwhile Ince delayed the release of *On the Night Stage* and passed *The Bargain* to another company, Famous Players, who, more impressed than Tom, released the film at once. It was an immediate success, and Ince quickly offered Hart a new contract. It was for one year at 125 dollars a week and allowing Bill to write his own scripts and assist in the direction of Western films.

Hart accepted the offer on the spot, not realising how paltry Ince's offer really was at a time when other film stars were getting salaries ranging between 1,000 and 2,000 dollars a week.

Hart whipped out eight two-reelers before Ince had time to release *On the Night Stage.*

It was at this time that the New York Motion Picture Company, Ince's studio, formed a new organization under the title of The Triangle Film Corporation. Tom was appointed one of the top producers, and Bill Hart, still under contract to Ince, was sensibly given his head by the new company. He was in his element, writing the sort of story in which he truly believed. His dedication in this respect shines through all his films, even to his last, *Tumbleweeds* (1925), when despite the fact that his movies were losing out in popularity before the success of Tom Mix and other flashy cowboys, the veteran stuck to his guns.

Although his work remains important in any review of Western films, his almost fanatical insistence on making his films

Now and then stars and starlets would take time out to disport themselves on the Californian beaches. Bill Hart cowers in the sand. Without his guns he was a push-over.

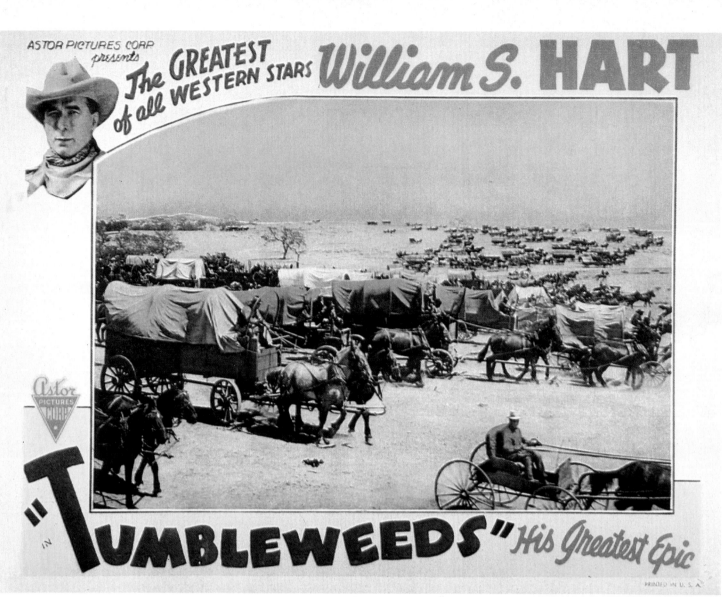

ASTOR PICTURES CORP
presents The GREATEST of all WESTERN STARS William S. HART

"TUMBLEWEEDS" His Greatest Epic

Above: Tumbleweeds, which went before the cameras in 1925, was not only William S. Hart's greatest epic, as this lobby card boasts, it was also his last. The film was outstanding for its gigantic hell-for-leather Oklahoma land rush sequences (W. S. Hart Tumbleweed Company).

Right: In 1925 Bill Hart produced Tumbleweeds for United Artists. Subsequently Hart took issue with the company over inadequate distribution and loss of profit. A well-nigh interminable lawsuit dragged on until 1950 when UA were compelled to pay $278,209 (W. S. Hart Tumbleweed Company).

16

true to life rendered them virtually out of date even when he started. The old West that he had personally known and loved was already a turned page in history.

Even so, Hart's contribution, alongside that of Broncho Billy Anderson, established the Western as one of Hollywood's great money-making genres.

Tumbleweeds was reissued in 1939 and for the last time Bill appeared before the cameras to film an emotional introduction which in effect was a lament for his great days of the past. He spoke for eight minutes.

'Oh, the thrill of it all,' he eulogized. Then fumbling clumsily with his sombrero, he turned tiredly away, back to retirement on his splendid ranch. It is today a public park.

William S. Hart reached the end of his life's trail seven years later on 23 June 1946. Ironically, this fervent exponent of the true Wild West is buried in the East, in Brooklyn.

Larger than Life: Tom Mix

The man who replaced William S. Hart in the affections of millions of filmgoers was of a completely different nature. If Hart was all dignity, then Thomas Edwin Mix was all impudence. Whereas Bill Hart would mow down his villainous enemies with his six-guns, Tom Mix was content to rope 'em in, sometimes even permitting them to ride away unpunished. In his films, Hart was a drinker, sometimes

Every inch the Western star, Tom Mix poses for a sombre studio portrait.

almost alcoholic, and smoked like a chimney. Mix never took a drink nor lit a cigarette. Hart rarely smiled, a frigid twitching of his lips sometimes expressing amusement. Mix laughed his way through all his features. Hart dressed in well-worn range clothes. Mix was an out-and-out dandy. Hart walked as though his riding boots were full of cement. Mix pranced and leaped as athletically as a ballet dancer.

Above all, Bill Hart presented the West very much as it actually was. Tom

Mix romped through a West that tended strongly to artificiality.

In one respect they *were* alike. They both loved horses and made heroes of them.

Tom Mix was born in Pennsylvania on 6 January 1880 and *not* near El Paso in Texas, as his 'official', i.e. studio, biographies maintained. Since on and off the screen Tom was larger than life, it followed in the minds of studio executives that his life before entering films must have been larger than life, too.

According to the publicity handouts, Tom Mix enlisted in the Army on 26 April 1898, the day after the United States declared war on Spain; posted to Cuba, he fought at the Battle of Guayamas where he was wounded in the neck; that war over, he battled in the Philippine Insurrection; then he journeyed to China in time to take a hand suppressing the Boxer Rebellion; a long hop took him to South Africa where, with no particular loyalty to either side, he fought successively for the British and the Boers; returning home, he donned the badge of a deputy sheriff and later served as a federal marshal and a Texas Ranger; in 1920 he was the owner of a large ranch which he lent out to film producers; eight years later he was rivalling William S. Hart as Hollywood's top cowboy film star.

Of this farrago, only the first and last statements and that which has him serving for a short time as some sort of lawman, a night marshal in Dewey, Oklahoma, appear to be true. Little is known of Tom's boyhood apart from his having attended school in Dubois, Pennsylvania and being fascinated, as naturally many boys were, by Buffalo Bill's Wild West Show.

Army records reveal that he enlisted on the date stated when he was eighteen, but nowhere is there any trace of his having been posted to Cuba. He served this first hitch in Delaware and Virginia, being honourably discharged in 1901 with the rank of sergeant.

Perhaps bored with civilian life, he was soon back in the army and shortly afterwards married for the first time. In all, he was to herd five charmers into holy wedlock's corral.

His first bride, née Grace Allin, took a dim view of most of her husband's time being taken up with matters military and launched an ultimatum, 'Me or the army!' Tom deserted from the army, the happy couple fleeing to Guthrie, Oklahoma. Grace took up teaching school and Tom became a physical fitness instructor, but the marriage soon fell apart and Tom took up a profession that would strengthen his good right arm – that of pulling up pints of beer for the thirsty customers of a saloon in Oklahoma City.

In 1905 Tom married Kitty Perrine, the saloon owner's daughter, and joined the Miller Brothers 101 Ranch at a monthly salary of 15 dollars and all found. As a

Right: Tom Mix was 47 years old when he starred in Outlaws of Red River *in 1927, but he was still playing the young hero and winning the heart of Margorie Daw (Fox Film Corporation).*

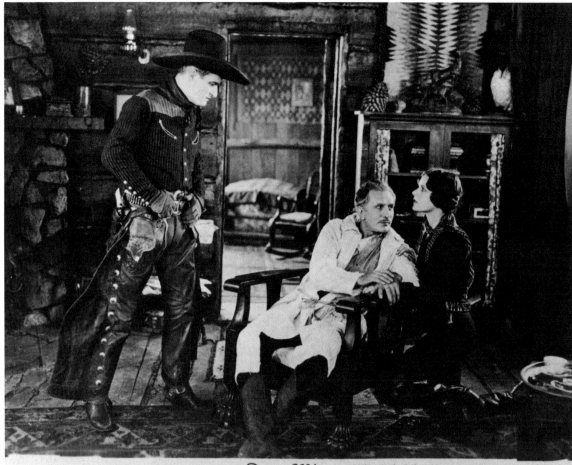

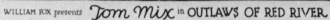

WILLIAM FOX presents *Tom Mix* in OUTLAWS OF RED RIVER

Below: The days of Tom Mix's skin-tight pants were still ahead of him when he played in In the Days of the Thundering Herd *in 1914 (Selig).*

youngster back in Pennsylvania, he had learned to ride well and to handle a lariat deftly so he could hold his own with the crew of experienced cowpokes already manning the Ranch.

His second marriage ran into difficulties and there followed another divorce. In 1909 Tom was ready to try his luck in double harness again, this time with Olive Stokes, a girl from Montana, with whom he was to remain for eight years.

In the same year Tom appeared before movie cameras for the first time. He had left the Miller Brothers for the Widerman Wild West Show in Amarillo, Texas, but had forsaken Texas to return to Oklahoma and the Will A. Dickey Circle D Ranch Wild West Show and Indian Congress.

It was here that he ran into William Selig who, having not so long before told Bill Hart that he was no longer interested in making Westerns, had changed his mind and was about to start work on a film entitled *Ranch Life in the Great South West* (1909) which was nothing more than

Anything goes, even eye-gouging, when Tom Mix swings into action in the 1927 movie The Broncho Twister. *The girl lurking in the background is Helene Costello, sister to the more famous Dolores (Fox Film Corporation).*

an exhausting round of rodeo acts – bull-dozing, roping, broncho-busting, fancy roping – all the fun and games.

Tom asked for and obtained a part in the feature, a fact confirmed by Selig's advertising posters on which Tom was billed as 'ex-US Marshal, expert rider and broncho-buster.'

For a few years Tom was on the Selig Polyscope Company pay-roll, during which time he played leading parts in several one-, two- and three-reelers. He also directed a number of these early efforts, concentrating on daring stunts and swift action, but as a director he was a good broncho-buster.

In 1918 a live-wire producer, real name William Fried, now William Fox, who had been watching and admiring Tom Mix's whirlwind style of present-ation, offered the cowboy actor 10,000 dollars a week – a far cry from the 150 dollars for which Tom had been working for Selig.

Given first-class directors such as John Ford and revelling in his undeniable flair for colourful showmanship, Tom was away like the proverbial arrow from a bow.

Gone were the gloom and Old Testa-ment moralizing, so much a part of the Bill Hart films. Gone, too, were the un-redeemed violence and bloodshed. Tom was all glamour and fun.

If the Mix films called for daring stunts, Tom was ever ready to carry them out himself. It has been estimated that during his film career, Tom Mix broke or cracked his ribs no fewer than twenty times. He broke an arm eight times and on six occasions broke a leg. Once falling heavily from his horse Tony, he shattered his shoulder and was *hors de combat* for several months.

'The King of the Cowboys' he was called and he lived up to the soubriquet. He had hundreds of extravagant suits, shirts, pants and boots all decorated with silver buckles, and wardrobes full of som-breros and fancy gun-belts. He drove huge custom-built cars which, in spite of the fact that he never took a drink in any of his pictures, were furnished with well-stocked bars. Not content with knowing that his name was in lights outside cin-emas across the world, he had a huge illuminated TOM MIX mounted on the roof of his Hollywood mansion.

His film-scripts were always carefully chosen and hand-tailored to suit his per-sonality, his directors and cameramen were of the best, the units that trailed from one Western location to another were all highly trained.

The coming of sound was to run down his career. He was never happy with 'those new-fangled contraptions', as he des-cribed the microphones. For the time being, outdoor films were a thing of the past, sound tending to drive production units into studios. Even so, Tom managed a few good talkies, amongst them *Destry Rides Again* (1932) and *My Pal the King* (1932) with Mickey Rooney. His last appearance in films was a serial *The Mir-acle Rider* (1935) and if it was slow-moving and thin on plot, at least it made over a million dollars for its producers, Mascot Pictures. From 1933 to 1950 'The Tom Mix Show' ran on radio keeping his name and image to the fore. He was also the first cowboy star to appreciate the value of giving his name to merchandise from toy six guns to scarves and breakfast cereals.

Opposite: Here is Tom Mix as he will always be remembered by his millions of fans, mounted on Tony and wearing his ten-gallon hat, tight-fitting breeches and rowelled Texan spurs.

Left: Tom Mix shows Claudia Dell how to handle a gun in one of his most celebrated movies, Destry Rides Again, *made in 1932 (Tom Mix Production/Universal).*

Carl Laemmle opened a nickelodeon in Chicago in 1909 when he was well-nigh penniless. Seven years later he was a wealthy movie producer and subsequently did more than any other producer to stimulate the Western genre. Here he is visiting Harry Carey during filming. Carl was always happy in the company of real-life cowboys.

Along the way, Tom had gained two daughters. He had also acquired two more wives, Victoria Forde and Mabel Ward, in 1918 and 1932 respectively.

By 1934 Tom was done with films and more wives. He bought an interest in the Sam B. Gill Circus, renamed it the Tom Mix Circus and, still the radiant showman, took off to enjoy himself, shooting, roping, riding, leaping from one side of a galloping horse to another like a veritable Spring-heeled Jack.

In 1939 while driving between Tucson and Phoenix, Arizona, he failed to take a corner and his car turned over. He escaped serious injury. There is no doubt it was a lucky escape. If it was not his first, it was his last. On 12 October 1940 at that self-same spot, Tom, who had been warned by a gas attendant to watch out for hazards ahead, struck a detour obstruction and his car turned over again. This time a metal suitcase he was transporting struck him, broke his neck and killed him instantly. He died as he had lived, at top speed.

The Quiet Man: Harry Carey

Quite different from Tom Mix in both his personal character and his films was Henry DeWitt Carey, better known in Movieland as Cheyenne Harry Carey.

Harry was born on 16 January 1878 in the Bronx, New York, the son of a New

York City Judge. He was educated at Hamilton Academy and New York University and, heading like his father for a law career, studied the intricacies of the legal profession until he was twenty-one. Then he was bowled over by a severe bout of pneumonia and sent to convalesce in Montana where, laid up, he put pen to paper and wrote a play.

It was not, as one might have expected, a melodrama of, say, a nail-biting murder trial in a New York courtroom. Its theme is pretty well summed up in its title, *Montana*. With rare aplomb, as soon as he was up and about, he produced his play himself and took the leading part. Un-expectedly to everyone but Harry, the play was a triumph.

He never returned to his law books, for *Montana* ran for five years on tour, no mean achievement. At the end of its run, Harry tried to repeat his success. From the romantic ranges of Montana, he transferred his scenario to the icy wastes of the Yukon in a play called *The Heart of Alaska* but it failed.

Undaunted, Harry forsook the stage for the movies. In 1909 he joined the American Biograph Company where he worked under the direction of David Wark (real name Lawrence) Griffith.

For the next six years Harry was to

The Scarlet Drop *was one of the many John Ford/Harry Carey movies made during Carey's Cheyenne Harry days. Molly Malone was his co-star in this film (Universal).*

slog away at one-reelers, not all of them Westerns. Then in 1914 he caught the discerning eye of the talent scouts of the Universal Film Manufacturing Company who proffered a contract and a salary of 1,500 dollars per week to make some short Westerns for them.

The director of this bunch was to be John Ford (real name Sean Aloysius Feeney) who, recently a prop boy for his more famous brother Francis, had been singled out by the boss of Universal, Carl Laemmle, and promoted. Now he was ready to begin a run of Westerns starring Harry Carey and all featuring the same hero, Cheyenne Harry, in the Broncho Billy tradition.

From then on Harry Carey's screen career was assured.

Never overly dramatic in the glowering Bill Hart sense of the word, he did not display the flamboyance of Tom Mix or Ken Maynard either. He usually appeared in the range clothes of real-life cowboys, check shirt and buckskin chaparejos. Down to earth, not especially handsome, always quietly spoken, he was expressive and gentle in feature and frequently flashed an infectious grin that appealed particularly to adult moviegoers.

His films were always strong on sentiment wherein, a chevalier of the boundless prairies, he would accord the ladies an old-world courtesy more reminiscent of the knights of old than the rough-and-ready frontiersmen. A favourite habit of his was to clasp his right arm with his left hand, a gesture that John Wayne was to imitate in the final shot of *The Searchers*, a John Ford film made in 1956. When Ford re-made *The Three Godfathers* in 1949, he included at the beginning of the film a dedication to Harry Carey, 'that bright star of the early Western sky'.

Harry was married to Olive Fuller Golden, a lovely actress who had appeared with him on various occasions, not least in the African-located *Trader Horn* (1931). Their son, Harry Carey Jr, Dobie to his friends, is today a well-known star having played in John Ford's *She Wore a Yellow Ribbon* (1949), *Rio Grande* (1950) and notably *The Searchers* (1956) in which Olive Carey played his mother. The Carey family were always close to John Ford's heart.

By the late 1920s, Harry was a front-rank Western star with more than 150 films strewn along the trail behind him. A wealthy man, he had settled down with his wife, son and daughter Ellen on a ranch in the San Fernando Valley.

Then at the peak of his success, disaster struck. The great St Francis dam broke and a raging flood swept across the valley, destroying the ranch and all its stock. Indomitably, he set about rebuild-

Opposite: Gabby Hayes, Julian Rivero and Harry Carey in The Night Rider *(Artclass Pictures, 1932).*

Below: Powdersmoke Range starred Harry Carey, Hoot Gibson, 'Big Boy' Williams, Tom Tyler and Bob Steele (RKO 1935).

Red River, *directed by Howard Hawks in 1948, was Harry Carey's last film (Monterey).*

ing the ranch, but ill-luck did not abandon him. Once again he lost his ranch, this time by fire.

Heavy of heart, he returned to the film studios. Many more notable movies lay ahead of him, among them *Powdersmoke Range* (1935), *The Shepherd of the Hills* (1941), *The Spoilers* (1942) and finally *Red*

River (1948), the last three being John Wayne features.

Already an ailing man with a weak heart, Carey survived only a few months after the completion of the film. He died on 21 September 1947 and they buried him in his black suit, high-heeled boots and black string tie.

Bright Stars of the Western Skies

Opposite: Unlike Tom Mix, whose battle record in the US Army was a figment of a publicity man's imagination, Buck Jones really did see action under fire in the Philippines in 1909. Fortunately the bad leg wound he sustained did not prevent him from becoming top bronco buster in a Wild West Show five years later. In Western Film annals Buck is ranked amongst the greatest. He died tragically in the Coconut Grove Night Club fire in 1942.

Towards the end of the 1920s sound was introduced to films. It proved a traumatic time for many film actors, in particular those foreigners whose command of English was very slight and those Americans whose voices and accents accorded ill with their movie images.

Amongst these latter was the great Tom Mix who lost his star status and never recovered it. Other Western stars avoided that fate, including Buck Jones, Tim McCoy, Hoot Gibson, Ken Maynard, Richard Dix and George O'Brien. John Wayne and Gary Cooper started to make their names during this decade but their 'glory days' were to come during the next.

Real-life Hero: Buck Jones

On the evening of 28 November 1942, that favourite Boston rendezvous of the famous, the Coconut Grove night-club, was in full swing. Suddenly fire broke out and in a matter of seconds flames raced through the building. Many diners were trapped.

The United States had been at war for nearly a year and many famous stars were touring the country selling war bonds. One of them was fifty-three-year-old Charles Frederick Gebhardt, known to the world as Buck Jones, star of more than 125 Western films. He was accompanied by his business manager and pardner from way back, Scott R. Dunlap, and both were being entertained by a bunch of New England film exhibitors in the Coconut Grove. When the alarm was raised Buck was dancing not far from the exit and made his escape. So did Scotty Dunlap, though his hands were badly burned. But the friends had become separated.

Buck, not seeing Scott, and heedless of his own safety, rushed back into the building to do what he could. He was taken from the collapsing ruins of the club, terribly burned and suffering from smoke inhalation.

He survived for only two days. So died a very gallant gentleman, mourned by his wife Odille, his son Charles, his daughter Maxine, married to Noah Beery Jr, and countless movie fans.

Sources differ as to the year of his birth. Sometimes it is quoted as 1888, sometimes as 1889 or 1891. It is highly likely that 1891 is the correct year.

He was born in Vincennes, Indiana and was only a youngster when his family moved to Red Rock, Oklahoma, where he learned to ride like a centaur and earned his nick-name Buck, short for Buckaroo.

Still only sixteen and fired with a lust for adventure, he enlisted in the US Army on 8 January 1907. His riding ability probably earned him his place in the US Cavalry. He cajoled his mother into signing his enlistment form, which stated falsely that he had been born 12 December 1888, so that the Army authorities would think that he was old enough to be recruited. Probably the confusion about Buck Jones' birth date arises from this.

Buck was wounded in the leg in the Philippines and was invalided home, just in time to spend Christmas with his folk.

As restless as ever, it was not long before he left his father's ranch for Indianapolis, already famous for its car-racing. His interest in automobiles had been aroused during his Army service and he managed to get a mechanic's job at the

Buck jones

Speedway. His wound now healed, he then signed on for another hitch with the Army. If he thought when he requested a transfer to the Aviation Squad that he could look forward to flying thrills, he was sadly mistaken. He was relegated to the lowly task of mechanic.

His term of service expiring on 23 October 1913, he left the Army for good and joined the Miller Brothers 101 Ranch. By the following year he was topping the bill as champion rider when the show played in New York.

Another rider for the 101 Ranch at the time was Odille Osborne. She and Buck fell in love and they were married on 11 August 1915. It was a romance that lasted Buck for the rest of his life. Twenty-seven years later as Buck lay on his death bed she wired him her last message, 'Love you'.

Buck and Dell, as his wife was called, settled down in Chicago. The Great War was convulsing the whole of Europe and Buck secured a job breaking horses for the Allies, a job that continued after the United States' entry into the War.

As soon as hostilities ceased, Buck and Dell hired their services out to the Ringling Brothers' Circus. The war might be over but there was still an aversion to German names, so Buck exchanged his name Gebhardt for Jones. Their joint salary was fifty dollars a week. It is fair to assume that Buck was not unaware of the success of that other one-time rider for the 101 Ranch, Tom Mix, who was currently in receipt of a weekly stipend of some 10,000 dollars. It would not have taken Buck long to figure out that what one buckaroo could do, so could another. Besides, Dell was expecting a child and that joint salary of fifty dollars was bound to be reduced, so the couple decided to drag pickets and take the trail to sunny Los Angeles. Buck sported twenty dollars for a clapped-out old auto and away they went.

In 1919 Tom Mix's producers, the

Buck Jones starred in six Westerns and one fifteen-episode serial during 1935. Outlawed Guns was one of the six (Buck Jones Productions).

Fox Film Corporation, took Buck Jones on as horse-breaker and stunt man. Working also for Fox was Scotty Dunlap and he and Buck struck up the friendship that was to last until that night at the Coconut Grove. Dunlap directed some of Buck's early oaters and in later years became his business manager. It was he who arranged Buck's last contract with Monogram when the star's popularity was waning.

Buck had been risking life and limb stunting for Tom Mix and Bill Hart and it was Tom who unknowingly set the stage for Buck's advent as a top star of Westerns. Tom, despite that 10,000 dollars a week, was still not satisfied that his services were being properly rewarded. Adopting in real life his future unpopular role of Dick Turpin, Tom presented Fox with his ultimatum: 'Deliver – or else!'

A short while previously Sol Wurtzel, Fox's production manager, had been urged by either Scotty Dunlap or William Farnum, a popular star of the time, to give

Buck a chance as an actor. The recommendation had resulted in a screen test and a contract. Buck's stuntman's salary of forty dollars a week was raised to one hundred and fifty.

Surprisingly, Buck's first film for Fox, *The Last Straw* (1920) was not located in the West, but his stunt work on Westerns had been matchless and it was remembered when William Fox, angered by Tom Mix's hold-up, looked round for a possible rival with whom to threaten his great star. He talked about raising Buck Jones to star status.

Mix refused to give way and, when all the chips were down, Fox knew that he couldn't let his top hand go, gave way himself and Tom was 7,500 dollars per week better off. Even so, he did not forget how Fox had tried to use Buck Jones against him and was Buck's sworn enemy until 1925 when Buck, now a fully-fledged film star in his own right and second only to Tom as a money-earner, played a bit

In the 1935 Stone of Silver Creek *Buck Jones owns a gambling saloon. An unknown is stealing his gold and Buck is determined to discover the culprit's identity. For such a mission, two guns are a great help (Buck Jones Productions).*

Buck Jones takes a flier from Silver's back to bust into a local den of iniquity. The film was Outlawed Guns, *a 1935 movie in which that old-time stalwart Pat O'Brien also appeared (Buck Jones Productions).*

part in *Dick Turpin*. He crossed swords with Tom Mix and when the mock duel ended so did the real one. Tom and Buck shook hands and were pals thereafter.

From 1920 until 1928 Buck Jones remained with Fox, making in all fifty-five Westerns, of varying quality. His acting ability was considerable and with cine-magoers his Western films attained a status second only to those of Mix. They abounded in the seasoning that Western fans demanded – break-neck action, good characterization, splendid photography and plenty of wide-open spaces.

Buck was a tall, broad-shouldered man with a square handsome face, a thin tight-lipped mouth and a strong determined jaw. His smile was comparatively rare but winning. Yet comedy was usually a strong

ingredient in his films. Even his villains sometimes were comic. If there is any criticism to be levelled at Buck's films, it is against those in which he took charge of production for it was then that he over-indulged his fun-loving humour. Your true Western fan wants hard-slugging quick-firing drama, not custard pies.

Buck had the good sense not to try to rival Tom Mix's sartorial splendour. He stuck to down-to-earth outfits with a minimum of decoration. Like Tom, he rode a much-loved horse, a grey by the name of Silver.

Buck's sojourn with Fox came to an end after he took his first holiday for years and came back to find that the Fox man-agement had reneged on their promise to pay his salary, still only a third of what

Left: Come one, come all! Buck Jones handles a couple of baddies with ease. A horse and cart were always useful for trundling vanquished wrong-doers to the city jail.

Below: Like all good Western heroes, Buck Jones regarded his horse Silver with great affection. Here it looks as though he's protecting his noble mount from sunstroke in a touching moment from Blood Will Tell, *a 1927 silent actioner (Fox Film Corporation).*

they were paying Mix, while he was away.

In a towering rage, Buck resigned and his long happy days with Fox were over. Rashly, he ventured into production and made a film called *The Big Hop* (1928) a Western with a difference for Buck harked back to the days when he was much taken with matters aeronautical and there were more flying stunts than six-guns and mustangs. *The Big Hop* was a big disaster and Buck was out of pocket to the tune of 50,000 dollars.

With rare courage, Buck gambled again, forming a Wild West show even though the great days of such spectacles were coming to an end. Inexperienced in such productions, he had to depend on the integrity of the 'experts' he hired. Expert they certainly were but only in directing Buck's money into their own saddle-bags, leaving Buck lighter by a quarter of a million dollars.

He had little choice but to turn back to movies. Luckily for him, Scotty Dunlap appeared with a welcome contract from Beverly Productions.

Talkies had now taken the film world by storm and many of the silent film stars had fallen from their places in the firmament. Buck's luck held for he had a splendidly modulated voice that accompanied his stalwart presence admirably and delighted the studio technicians. Of all the cowboy stars of silent films, he was the only one to continue in the big time and when Columbia bought his contract from Beverly in 1931 he was once more riding high.

For the next seven years all his films – fifty, plus six serials, one of twelve episodes and five of fifteen – were moneymakers, but by 1938 the yodelling guitar-strumming duo, Gene Autry and Roy Rogers, were ousting the two-gun two-fisted close-mouthed saddle-hawks from their long enjoyed supremacy. Even John Wayne, only thirty-one years old but with forty movies already behind him, was suffering an eclipse despite his forlorn attempt to croon as Singin' Sandy in *Riders of Destiny* (1933). Buck Jones was ranked third in a poll of cowboy stars but that did not prevent his studio from refusing to renew his contract.

From then on, his career was one of ups and down, culminating in the form-

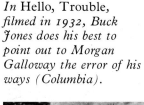

In Hello, Trouble, *filmed in 1932, Buck Jones does his best to point out to Morgan Galloway the error of his ways (Columbia).*

ation of a new company headed by Buck and Scotty Dunlap. They launched a series concerning the adventures of three pards of the prairie called 'The Rough Riders'. Buck was one, Tim McCoy and light-relief Raymond Hatton the others.

In all, eight very profitable 'Rough Riders' films were made. But the United States was now at war and Tim McCoy joined the army while Buck and Scotty set off on the ill-fated bond-selling tour that was to end with Buck's tragic death.

Today the memory of Buck Jones is still firmly entrenched in the hearts of those Western fans who remember his films and the quiet genial simplicity that radiated from the real-life hero who lost his life while trying to save others.

The Man Trailer, *vintage 1934, was Buck Jones' last film for Columbia. It was a remake of* The Lone Rider *which, in turn, was a rehash of W. S. Hart's well-known* The Return of Draw Egan *(Columbia).*

The Red Man's Friend: Colonel Tim McCoy

Jesse Lasky's epic Western of 1923, *The Covered Wagon*, was a blockbuster, a huge box-office success at a time when Westerns were apparently becoming unpopular with filmgoers – a fact which made the enormous budget of half a million dollars appropriated to it seem a gamble indeed on the part of its producers, Famous Players-Lasky (President: Alfred Zukor). One of the thousands of extras hired for the film lucky enough to make good out of it was Colonel Tim McCoy.

To man the wagon train that was to toil its way across Snake Valley, Nevada, where *The Covered Wagon* was to be shot, a small army of extras was recruited. To

Clad in natty riding breeches, Colonel Tim McCoy takes stock of himself in a studio mirror.

Lois Wilson, seen here in The Covered Wagon *later starred with Richard Dix in* To the Last Man *and* The Vanishing American *(Famous Players-Lasky).*

attack the wagon train hundreds of real Indians were needed to ride the vast herd of horses and ponies that had been assembled.

Jesse Lasky wrote to the Board of Indian Commissioners for help. It arrived in the form of a tall handsome man in immaculate army uniform, an adjutant general of Wyoming, one Colonel Timothy J. F. McCoy.

He was born on 10 April 1891 in Saganaw, Michigan, the youngest of the three sons of the Chief of Police. In 1907 he was attending a Jesuit college in Chicago when the Miller Brothers 101 Ranch Wild West Show arrived. The show ran for seven nights and Tim sat with beating heart and fired with the lust for adventure at every performance.

One morning he packed a bag, quit school forever and boarded a train bound for Omaha, heading for adventures in a West that was still wild and woolly. En route he was advised to drop off at Lander, Wyoming, good horse country.

McCoy obtained work on horse ranches, generally helping in any of the menial tasks that abounded. He eventually learned to ride well, cursed his saddle-sores and at last became a fully-fledged bronchobuster. During these early years, he sensibly saved his money until he had enough to buy a small section of land. He had fallen in love with Wyoming and indeed maintained a home there for forty years.

Fascinated by the lore and customs of the Indians, he spent much time on the Wind River reservation where the Arapahoe and Shoshone tribes lived and soon formed an affinity with these ex-nomads for whom the free life on the Great Plains had gone forever. In return they took him to their hearts. He was adopted by the Arapahoes and given the Indian cognomen 'High Eagle'.

Tim learned the spoken and sign lan-

guages of these reservation Indians. He also absorbed the more subtle facial expressions and physical gestures which even today are so much a part of Indian emotional communication. It was this knowledge that was ultimately to launch Tim on his movie career.

He was twenty-six when America went to war in 1917. He applied for enrolment in the Officers' Candidate School, was accepted and duly commissioned as captain of cavalry. Later he transferred to the artillery.

He was decorated on a number of occasions for gallantry and when the war ended he was posted to Wyoming with the rank of brigadier, to act as adjutant general. His ex-commanding officer, Major General Hugh Scott, was appointed head of the Board of Indian Commissioners. Scott, like Tim, was a fluent linguist in the

Indian tongue and well practised in the sign language.

When the Board of Indian Commissioners received Jesse Lasky's call for help in the production of *The Covered Wagon*, it is fair to believe that it was Hugh Scott who had something to do with Tim's being sent to the studio.

There, Lasky succinctly outlined to Tim his requirements and Tim, in true old-time cavalry fashion, charged into the fray. As he afterwards related, 'I gathered together two train-loads of Indians, bucks, squaws, papooses, tepees, dogs, everything.'

It became Tim's job to take care of this motley conglomeration, not only to translate the director's complicated instructions but also to quench the blood-thirst of sundry braves who, with memories of the not-so-distant past resurrected,

Opposite: The Covered Wagon *of 1923 was the first Western epic, with* J. Warren Kerrigan *and* Lois Wilson *as the stars (Famous Players-Lasky).*

Below: Tim McCoy takes time out during the filming of Sioux Blood *in 1928 to explain to a couple of painted warriors the intricacies of a movie camera (Metro-Goldwyn-Mayer Pictures).*

Right: Tim McCoy cuddles a canine companion in The Indians Are Coming, *a thrill-a-minute serial that had kids leaping out of their seats during Saturday Matinées way back in 1930 (Universal).*

Below: Although Buck Jones played the lead in Arizona Bound, *Tim McCoy was always more than ready to take over the gun-play as this scene bears witness (Monogram 1941).*

now and then itched to raise a few scalps. Lois Wilson, playing the long-suffering heroine, recounts how one enthusiastic warrior, a marksman with bow and arrow, having learned that she was supposed to be wounded during an Indian attack, happily offered to shoot her right through the shoulder and 'not break bone, not hurt much', an offer that Miss Wilson understandably rejected.

Tim's assistance was of such value that when the film was completed, the studio were reluctant to let him go. He was offered a part in the filming of Zane Grey's *The Thundering Herd* (1925). In the cast were Jack Holt, then a big star, Lois Wilson and, way down at the bottom of the list, a newcomer, real name Frank James Cooper, rechristened Gary by his agent.

Shortly afterwards Tim was to meet up with Lois Wilson again when he acted as technical adviser on another Zane Grey-inspired film *The Vanishing American* (1925) with Richard Dix in the lead.

Meanwhile Metro-Goldwyn-Mayer talent scouts justified their salaries by bringing to their studio's attention the filmic attractions of the tall lithe man who knew so much about the true West. What followed was a contract for Tim who was at once starred in a series of well-produced MGM Westerns which ended in 1929. That clipped voice of his easily passed the silents-to-talkies hurdle and from then on he starred for many companies – Universal, Columbia, Puritan Films, Victory Pictures and Monogram – in more than sixty sagebrushers. As already related, his last eight films prior to the outbreak of World War II were the 'Rough Riders' series with Buck Jones.

Still imbued with ardent patriotism and despite his fifty-one years, Tim re-enlisted in the army for active duty. With the rank of Lieutenant-Colonel his request for action was approved and the hardy veteran went forth again to war. Officers were needed to liaise between ground and air tactical units and Tim was posted to such duties. Happily he emerged unscathed at the end of the war, having collected yet more awards for bravery.

Those decorations became known to Mike Todd who remembered them when in 1956 he cast Tim as the leader of a cavalry squadron which rode to David Niven's rescue in *Around the World in 80 Days*. When the film ended production, Mike handsomely presented Tim with a

When Phineas Fogg, who is trying to beat the clock in Around the World in 80 Days, *has to be rescued from the hands of marauding Indians, he is saved by none other than Colonel Tim McCoy, brought out of retirement by Mike Todd in 1956, once again to lead the US Cavalry (London Films-Michael Todd Productions).*

Right: Requiem for a Gunfighter *was a fitting title for this, Tim McCoy's last film. In it he played a circuit judge and to ensure that the movie – made in 1965 when Tim was 74 – was a winner, several other top Western stars, among them Bob Steele, Johnny Mack Brown and Rod Cameron, joined the cast* (Premiere Productions)*.*

complete set of the thirteen campaign medals and decorations for bravery in action in two World Wars.

The following year Tim played the part of another army officer, this time General Allen, minus a right arm, in *Run of the Arrow* which starred Rod Steiger. Playing a glowering young Indian was fledgling Charles Bronson.

Tim McCoy appeared in his last film, *Requiem for a Gunfighter*, in 1965. It was a cameo part as a circuit judge but if the film world thought that he was done with boots and saddle he merrily corrected their opinion by starting a new lease of life, shooting, riding, cracking a bull-whip and spinning lariats and yarns in the Wild West section of a touring show entitled Tommy Scott's Country Music Caravan.

At eighty he was still riding with the best of them.

Tim married twice, firstly in 1921 to Agnes Miller, by whom he had two sons and a daughter. The marriage ended in divorce in 1931 and fourteen years later he was married again, to Inga Arvad who presented him with two sons. He was widowed in 1974 and survived his wife until 1978 when he died peacefully on 29 January in Nogales, Arizona. His body today lies where his heart had dwelt since early boyhood, in the Western lands.

Rompin', stompin': Hoot Gibson

Opposite: In the 1920s, Hoot Gibson, seen here with one of his favourite mounts, Mutt, was a top Western star. It couldn't have been easy during the course of seven days to spend a weekly salary of $14,000 but Hoot managed it every week as long as his contract existed. This achievement might have been one of the reasons why he died broke in 1962.

At the corner of Cahuenga and Hollywood Boulevards there once stood a cafe-cum-saloon called by its thirsty clients the Waterhole. Any newcomer entering there for a quiet drink might well have been astonished to find himself in the centre of a yelling mob of cowboys urging on to greater efforts two brawling youngsters engaged in a Homeric fist-fight. The taller of these fistical gents would have been, more likely than not, a grinning cowpoke, two inches under six feet in height, bulky, fair-haired and blue-eyed, his none-too-handsome features bruised from previous encounters.

A big-time gambler receiving the red-carpet treatment at a certain lush hotel on the Las Vegas Strip forty years later would have been intrigued to see a one-time famous movie star, his fight-worn face now further disfigured by the scars of a near-fatal air crash, step forward and greet him officially with an infectious smile.

The brawler of the Waterhole and the friendly greeter of the Las Vegas hotel were one and the same, a movie star who during the period separating these two occasions in his chequered career had made and lost a fortune, at one time earning as much as 14,500 dollars in one week and this when ten dollars weekly was regarded by the ordinary working man as a good salary.

His name was Charles Edmund Gibson, known to the world as Hoot Gibson, a top star of Western movies, although it should be added that while on the one hand he was one of the most popular cowboy actors, he only made the Motion Picture Herald's national poll once, and that was in ninth place, in 1936 when his heyday was almost at an end.

Why the singular nickname? One ex-

planation given is that he was so dubbed because as a kid his favourite pastime was hunting owls. Another is that he was branded 'Hoot' when riding a bicycle in the employ of the Owl Drug Company in Los Angeles. Whatever the truth, he was already well-known to everyone as Hoot Gibson when he was twenty and won the title of All-Around Champion Cowboy in a contest at the Pendleton Round-up in Oregon in 1912, a title that Ken Maynard was also to win in 1919.

Hoot was born in Tekamah, Nebraska on 6 August 1892. Conflicting accounts exist about his early boyhood. According to one, he ran away from home at the age of thirteen to join the Miller Brothers 101 Ranch at Fort Bliss, Oklahoma. In 1907, the story goes, he signed a four-year contract with the Dick Stanley-Bud Atkinson Wild West Show, touring in the States and Australia.

Another report has it that he lived in Tekamah until 1907, working for local farms and then went to California to join his sick mother who had gone there to regain her health. It confirms that he later joined the Stanley-Atkinson Show, but in 1910.

Whichever is correct, it seems certain that he was with the Stanley-Atkinson bunch in 1910 because that is where he met another wild spirit named Artemus Ward Acord, two years younger than Hoot and twice as hare-brained.

Still legendary are the battles that these two fighting fools enjoyed, especially in their favourite venue, the Waterhole. Here young cowboys would congregate, drink, gamble, gossip and quarrel while waiting for a summons to any studio where a Western was currently being filmed. When Universal, for example, wanted a posse or an outlaw gang, a white flag would be run up to the top of the studio flagpole. Then would follow a mad scramble to the wiry ponies hitched outside the bar and a headlong gallop to reach

the studio first. The pay was good – five dollars a day. Ranchers at that time were paying their cowhands forty to fifty dollars a month.

Cowboys were to be seen in strength at the Waterhole in wintertime, for during spring and summer they could find plenty of work risking their necks in rodeos or Wild West shows, while in the fall, they would adjourn to their true vocation of rounding up longhorn steers on the big ranches.

The habituees of the Waterhole were mostly young wild-and-woollies, for ranchers tended to keep the older long-service men during the winter and let the young bloods go. They were transient workers at the best of times and it was a happy-go-lucky existence that appealed to those footloose teenagers and to none more so than those rompin', stompin', no-holds-barred sons of the saddle, Hoot Gibson and Art Acord.

Both were lowly extras when they were signed on by the Biograph Company in 1910 to participate in a Western *Two Brothers* which was being filmed in San Juan, Capistrano. Both were called upon to double for the stars and chance their luck in death-defying stunts. The intrepid

Art Acord was once called upon to make his horse rear until it toppled back on him, a fall that has killed many a rider before and since. Luckily for Art, he lived to tell the tale.

Two years later in Pendleton, Oregon, where Hoot had gone to compete in the Round-up Rodeo, he met a pretty girl, Helen Wenger, a star rodeo rider. They fell in love and were to stay that way for the next nine years.

Helen was to become a film star in her own right, under her adopted name Helen Gibson. It was naturally assumed that she and Hoot were married. He always contended that they had started living together in Pendleton because lodgings were so scarce that the only chance of obtaining a room was to present themselves as husband and wife, married couples being given preference. Hoot's implication was that he and Helen were never married although she, for her part, always stoutly maintained that they were.

It was when Hoot met young Jack Ford, the director, that he started on the trail that was to take him to the heady heights of stardom. It began in 1915 when Universal figured that Hoot was just about the right idiot to gallop his pony

Opposite: Mountie Art Acord comes to the aid of Esther Ralston in Gypsy Trail, *made in 1918 by Paramount. In the 1933 version of* To the Last Man *with Randolph Scott, Esther was called upon to swim in the nude. The scene failed to create the furore Hedy Lamarr caused when she appeared in the buff in* Ecstasy, *also filmed in 1933.*

Below: Flaming Frontier *was filmed in 1926. Anne Cornwall behind Harold Goodwin is looking back over her shoulder toward a contrite Hoot Gibson. Goodwin, a tall handsome actor, specialized in sneaky roles (Universal).*

over cliff edges, roly-poly with his mount down mountain sides, jump chasms, gallop through burning buildings or perform any of the other deeds of derring-do that seemed in those days so frequently to befall the celluloid riders of the West.

Jack Ford was directing Harry Carey in a series of sagebrushers and Hoot doubled for Harry. It was the beginning of a life-long friendship for the three of them.

Two years passed while Hoot progressed to second lead with Harry Carey in *Straight Shooting* (1917), and could look forward to playing a leading part soon, but the States was now at war and Hoot and his old sparring partner Art Acord reckoned that the sooner two guys who knew what fighting was really about took a hand in the general scrimmage, the sooner it would be over. They enlisted and served together in the US Tank Corps. Art was awarded the Croix de Guerre and Hoot, like Tim McCoy, was decorated for bravery in action several times.

The two heroes returned to Hol-

lywood, intent on recommencing their movie careers. Art, who had won the 1912 title of World Champion Bulldogger and proved his fighting prowess on bar-room floors and distant battlefields, was also a fellow apparently determined to drink strong spirits faster than the distilleries could churn them out.

In spite of his brawling and alcoholism, he appeared in a number of Western serials, one at least of which won critical applause, and some two-reelers. But it couldn't last. Finally drink and drugs won out and he died in Chihuahua, Mexico in 1931, reportedly a suicide, having swallowed cyanide. His friends, though, would have none of this. 'He was knifed in a bar by a no-good Mexican vaquero,' was one succinct verdict.

Unlike Acord, Hoot could slap a curb on his unruly nature and after his return from France, started to roll out a long series of two-reel Westerns, several of them directed by himself. His average was one per month.

Of them all – there were about eight –

only three were directed by John Ford but significantly it was he who directed Hoot in his first feature length film *Action* (1921) which catapulted him into stardom. In the same year Hoot married Helen Johnson, a vaudeville performer, so unless he was committing bigamy he must have obtained a divorce from his previous wife. Either that, or he and Helen Gibson were never married. Hoot, like Tom Mix, was a much married man; there were two more weddings ahead of him.

Action was his reward for winning an amazing popularity in his two-reelers. He had been quick to see that there was a place for films that would appeal to children as much as to adults. To this end, his scripts were uncomplicated, brim-full of fantastic trick-riding, stunts and comedy. The characters he played were usually down-to-earth, easy going and humorous and instead of forcing the pace, a driving masterful hero, he was a victim of unlucky misadventures for which he was not responsible, a sort of Johnny-on-the-spot

seemingly waiting for the world to fall in on him. Add to this his boyish grin and one can understand why in the cynical Jazz Age he became one of its best loved actors.

With youthful audiences in mind, he did not wish to convey an unhealthy admiration for the art of gun play and seldom carried a gun on his hip. Only at crisis point was he likely to take a gun in hand and then usually he had to scoop up a gun dropped by a baddie or borrow one from a friend. On the comparatively few occasions that he *did* wear a gun it would be thrust rather inconspicuously in his belt or in the top of his riding boot. Interestingly, in *The White Buffalo* made in 1977, Charles Bronson as Wild Bill Hickok at one point carries his guns stuffed into the tops of his boots.

From 1921, the year of *Action*, Hoot sped from one film to another, confidently bridging the gap between silents and talkies until 1937 when he rode through twelve episodes of a serial *The Painted*

Did that toughie on the left pass a slighting remark about Hoot Gibson's fancy footwear? Be that as it may, the argument has reached The Boiling Point *in the 1932 film of that title (Universal).*

Above: Hoot Gibson relaxing off set with director John Ford.

Opposite: In 1937 when Ken Maynard filmed Boots of Destiny *he was a top-ranking Western star. The film was a routine oater once again highlighted by Ken's amazing riding dexterity.*

Stallion. There followed a six-year interim during which time he toured with a circus. Then in 1943 he was riding the celluloid trail again, appearing with Ken Maynard in 'The Trail Blazers' series, produced by Monogram.

Ken and Hoot were old buddies, sharing an enthusiasm for flying. Hoot had been racing against Ken over Los Angeles airport in 1933 when he crashed and was very fortunate to escape with his life.

When 'The Trail Blazers' was produced Ken was already over the hill and seeking solace in the bottle. One bender too many and he was out of the series after completing five films, but Hoot continued with the able assistance of Bob Steele until 1944 when the series was wound up.

His marriage to film actress Sally Eilers, his second (? third) wife, was over and he was now married for the last time to Dorothy Dunstan, a singing rodeo rider.

It was all downhill for Hoot now. He did not appear in another film until 1959 when John Ford cast him as a cavalry sergeant in John Wayne's *The Horse Soldiers* (1959). The perky grin was still there, albeit he was now of considerable girth. He appeared briefly the next year in *Oceans Eleven* (1960) with Frank Sinatra but that was his last film.

For a time, he continued with his congenial occupation of hotel greeter in Las Vegas, but in 1962 he was languishing in the Motion Picture Country Home and Hospital in California, stricken with stomach cancer. He died on 23 August.

The Fiddling Buckaroo: Ken Maynard

Who was the first song-bird of the saddle? Gene Autry? Roy Rogers? Dick Foran? What about John Wayne in his role of Singin' Sandy in *Riders of Destiny* made in 1933? But then Big John didn't actually sing. The warbling was done for him by a singer named Smith Ballew. No, the honours probably go to Ken Maynard. A man of many accomplishments, he could play the piano, the violin, the banjo and the guitar. He sang reasonably well and could give a very agreeable performance when accompanying himself on the fiddle.

Ken was a fore-runner in introducing suitable – as well as unsuitable – musical scores to Western films. His taste ran from folksy cowboy songs to sepulchral classics, often quite inappropriate to mesquite-and-cactus sagas.

Musician he might have been but his marvellous horsemanship was the key that was to open the door to film stardom and fabulous salaries. Tom Mix, Buck Jones, Hoot Gibson, all were superb riders but Ken Maynard out-shone them all. In the saddle he was capable of the most astonishing athletic feats at headlong gallops. He was so powerful that at top speed he could reach down from his horse, grab a cowboy lying, supposedly unconscious, in the path of a cattle stampede, hoist him up behind and carry him off to safety. Only a horseman of consummate skill and herculean strength could have carried out such a feat.

Ken was born on 21 July 1895 in

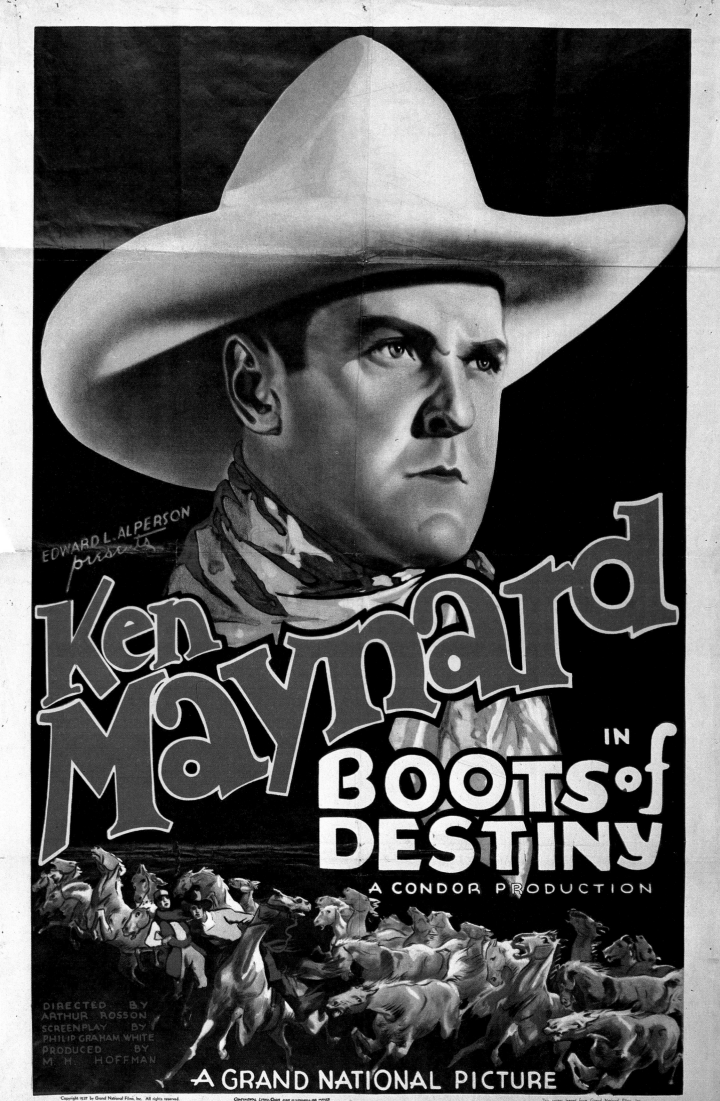

Vevey, Indiana. He was the eldest of five children, his brother Kermit, who also became a well-known cowboy star, being the youngest. Their father was the proprietor of a small construction company but Ken, even at school, wanted no part of that. He was twelve when he ran off to join a wagon show. His irate father brought him back home but Ken was already converted to the notion that there's no business like show business.

In 1911 he obtained his parents' permission to join a touring carnival. Two years later he was with Buffalo Bill's Wild

West Show, the next year with Kit Carson's Wild West and twelve months afterwards with another show, that of Hagenbeck and Wallace.

He was all set for a future with Wild West shows but along came the Great War and he enlisted. He was posted to Camp Knox, Kentucky as a civil engineer, an indication that even at this early age – he was twenty-two – he was not just another rodeo rider and good for nothing else. While he was in Kentucky he married, but details regarding who and when are sparse.

In 1919 he was out of the army and back with Hagenbeck and Wallace. Then followed a short spell with Pawnee Bill's Show, after which he was off to Oregon and the Pendleton Rodeo, winning the proud title of All-Around Champion of the World, previously held, it will be remembered, by Hoot Gibson back in 1912. Ken also won 42,000 dollars, the prize that went with the title.

Two years later in 1921, he was with the Ringling Brothers' Circus in Los Angeles, receiving 40,000 dollars a year. It was then that a friend, it might have been Buck Jones or Tom Mix, for Ken knew them both, introduced him to Lynn Reynolds who was directing some of Tom's movies.

He was given a screen test which pleased the bosses at Fox and was signed on for 100 dollars a week, a long way short of the 40,000 dollars a year the Ringling Brothers were paying him. Ken was taking a chance but he knew that he could ride better than Tom Mix and Buck Jones. All he had to do, therefore, was to act better than either of them, too. This he never did, for while he was no better an actor than Tom, Buck was certainly superior to Ken.

He was given a few small parts but he made no specific progress until 1923 when William Randolph Hearst, the newspaper magnate who was besotted with the lovely blonde actress Marion Davies, threw a pile of money into producing for her *Janice Meredith*, a film with an American Revolution background. In it, Paul Revere was to ride again bringing his midnight warning to the patriots that 'The redcoats are coming! To arms! To arms!' The man who played the part had to be a spectacular horseman.

Ken Maynard may not have made a particular mark as an actor but in the saddle no-one could match him. He obtained the part, received commendable notices and from then on, for the next twenty years, his name appeared above the title of all the eighty-six Western films he made.

During his years as a film star, Ken Maynard worked for several producers. He started with the Davis Distributing Corporation and went on to make films for twelve other companies, amongst them Universal, Columbia and Grand National.

All his films were showcases for his amazing feats of horsemanship, usually on his magnificent palomino, Tarzan, called the Wonder Horse. It was no misnomer, for the beautiful animal was the most sagacious of all the movie mounts. It was almost as though the horse knew what acting was all about.

Tarzan was called upon to perform the most eye-boggling tricks; he could pirouette, hobble along on his hind legs, fall down and play 'dead' and had he been required to stand on his head would doubtless have made a sterling attempt.

He even had his own fan club; surely there would be few to dispute the title of Wonder Horse. He served Ken well for his purchase price of fifty dollars.

When Ken divorced his second wife Jeanne, whom he had married in 1923, he married again, this time Mary Leeper from Indiana. He was to stay with her for the next ten years, the best of his life.

In 1930 Ken made some good films for Universal and then went off to other producers for three years. Despite his now burgeoning reputation for an almost maniacal temper, an over-bearing disposition and a seemingly unquenchable thirst for John Barleycorn, Carl Laemmle, the guiding light of Universal, in 1933 invited Ken to return with a quite splendid offer – not only a salary of 10,000 dollars for each week's shooting but also a virtually unlimited control on his films. As unrestrained as ever, Ken failed to keep a tight control on the financing of his films, and a second parting with Universal resulted.

In Death Rides the Range *Fay McKenzie does her best to prevent Ken Maynard dishing out the sort of punishment that veteran badman Charles King was accustomed to in most of his movies (Colony).*

Opposite: Unkind critics were wont to remark that in many ways Tarzan the Wonder Horse was a better actor than his master, Ken Maynard.

Below: Strawberry Roan *was quite possibly the most celebrated movie Ken Maynard made for Universal in 1933 if only for the fact that it contained a song later made famous by Gene Autry in his own 1948 film* The Strawberry Roan.

Ken was not so reckless as he had been. He needed a stand-in now and there was nobody more suitable than his brother Kermit who had been acting in a few rather modest oaters for an independent company and was now 'resting'. So Kermit joined his brother, but friction followed for while Ken was a dedicated tippler, Kermit was a teetotaller.

Their arguments ended in a monumental bar-brawl and thereafter they rarely spoke to each other.

Then a row flared up with Carl Laemmle's son, who had been carefully watching Ken's activities. The star had grossly exceeded the financial appropriation for his latest movie, a bad one. Its title was *Smoking Guns* (1934) and Ken was smoking with fury when he received a summons to the office of Laemmle Senior, there to be rebuffed for his delinquencies. Ken stamped out of the office, never to work for Universal again and never again to have the film-making freedom that he had enjoyed there.

Nat Levine of Mascot Pictures next approached Ken with a proposal to star in a new series of musical Westerns. Nat had recently signed up a warbler who had been singing for a Chicago radio station. His name was Gene Autry and Nat wanted to try him out, wisely with a top star heading the cast.

Ken was over the hill now and his third marriage was breaking up. Throughout the first film *In Old Santa Fe* (1934) Ken furiously rounded on the director many times, even threatening to shoot him on one occasion. He insulted his leading lady, Evelyn Knapp, and anybody else who dared to cross his path. His behaviour during the follow-up, a twelve-episode serial, *Mystery Mountain* (1934), was insupportable and when shooting was over, Nat Levine indicated to Ken that in the interests of future tranquillity and good relations at the studio and on the lot, Ken would have to go.

He was lucky enough to be hired by Columbia to make four Westerns, but it was a saddle-weary man who now rode the Hollywood hills. When he ran out of

Right: When Smoking Guns *was scheduled for 1934 by Universal, Ken Maynard was already drinking heavily, violently quarrelsome and parting from his wife.*

UNIVERSAL presents *Ken Maynard in* SMOKING GUNS

Opposite: At least when Richard Dix, normally clean-shaven, played the part of Wild Bill Hickok in 1941 in Badlands of Dakota, *he was not averse to sporting a Wild Bill moustache. Two other stars, William S. Hart and Gary Cooper, abjured such facial adornment when they played Wild Bill (Universal).*

mileage with Columbia, he organized the Ken Maynard Diamond K Ranch and Wild West Circus. The show was a disaster, such a flop that it only ran for two weeks and lost thousands of dollars, so Ken went back to filming. Four films for Grand National and four for Colony were followed by six 'Trail Blazers' pictures with Hoot Gibson and Bob Steele. Ken's last film was *Harmony Trail* (1944, released 1947), financed by a small outfit, Mattox Productions.

Ken was now running to seed. He was fleshy, paunchy, his stomach overhanging his gun-belt. Too unreliable for another studio, big or small, to hire him, he went back to what he could do best – riding.

His name could still attract crowds to the circuses and rodeos in which he appeared. Even now he was capable of those breath-taking stunts and trick-riding that had won him fame and fortune.

But nothing lasts forever. Ken could no more hold on to fame than he could to fortune. He had married yet again, this time to Bertha Denham, who had caught his eye while she was swinging on a trapeze for the Ringling Brothers' Circus. When she died in 1968, Ken was alone in the world. None of his marriages had produced a child. He was seventy-three and from then on he lived in a trailer in the San Fernando Valley, his only companions the bottles that had cursed him all his life. His only income apart from his retirement pay was the royalties accruing from the paperback Westerns he wrote as Bliss Lomax.

Finally, a geriatric, he was taken to the Motion Picture Country Hospital where he died on 23 March 1973. His place in the Cowboy Hall of Fame is secure, this tragic man who, blessed with so many talents, could never restrain himself, not even when it came to drinking himself into oblivion.

Strong and Silent: Richard Dix

Compared with Hoot Gibson's one hundred and twenty-four Westerns, Richard Dix's eighteen actioners look somewhat inauspicious at first glance. Short though the list is, it includes some excellent Westerns, and it is generally agreed that even though most of his films were *not* Westerns, Dix must be ranked among the top exponents of the Western hero.

All his Westerns were feature films

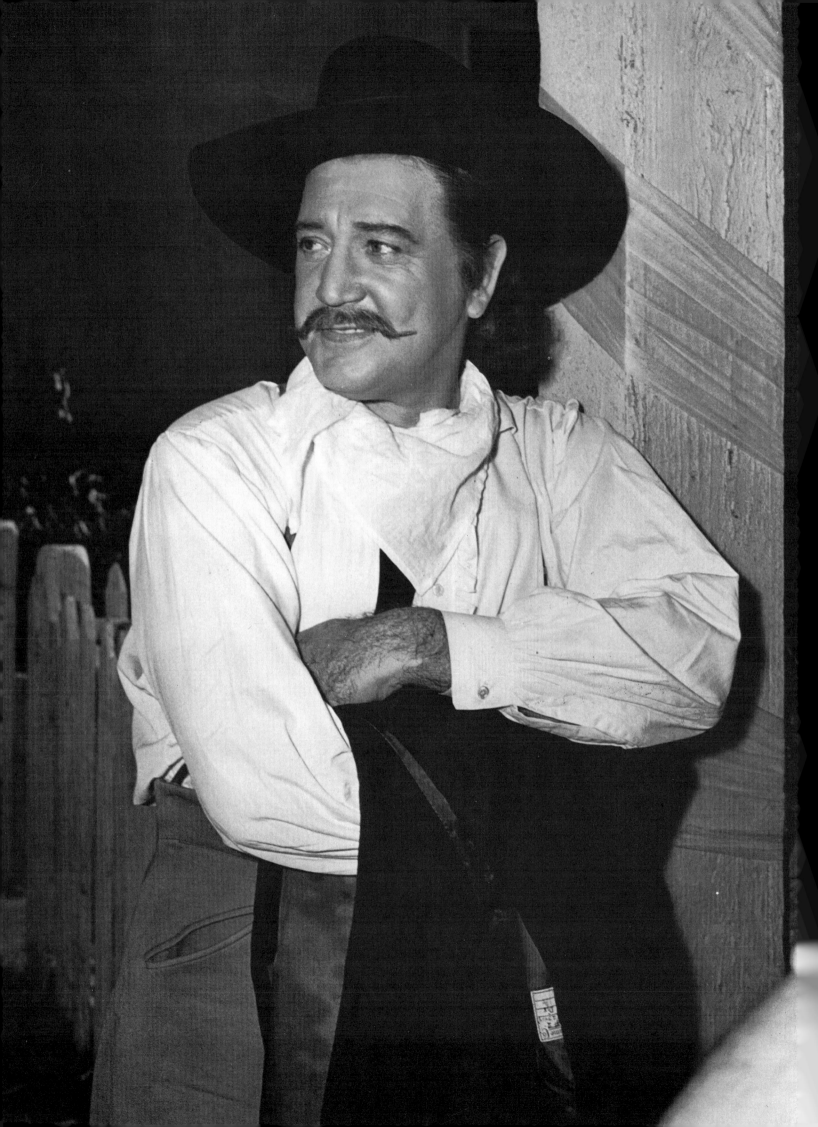

and two of them – *The Vanishing American* (1925) and *Cimarron* (1931) – are landmarks in the all-time cavalcade of Western films. *Cimarron* was the only film concerning the West to have won the coveted prize of the Academy Awards' Best Film of the Year. Dix and his co-star Irene Dunne were both nominated for the best actor and actress awards.

He was born Ernest Carlton Brimmer on 18 July 1894, and when the studio publicists came to write about him he proudly pointed to the fact that he could trace his ancestry back to one of the dauntless pilgrims who sailed to the New World in the gallant and all-but-legendary *Mayflower.*

Unlike Tom Mix, Buck Jones, Tim McCoy and Hoot Gibson, he did not come to Hollywood from cattle ranges or rodeo circuits, but via stock companies and the Broadway stage. Born in St Paul, Minnesota, he was educated at North Western College and the University of Minnesota

Medical School and was easily attracted to the amateur dramatics practised at the seminaries.

He caught the attention of a touring company who offered him a role in one of their productions, *Richelieu*. He was all for joining and taking off into the dreary world of travelling theatrics but his parents took a dim view of such adolescent notions, and persuaded him to continue his medical studies.

That resolute chin of his truly betokened a determined nature, however, and young Ernest kept a watchful eye open for any more opportunities. One presented itself when another touring company in town, needing someone to act a football player, gave him the part.

This second opportunity finally convinced the young man that acting was for him. He learned his trade the hard way, acting in stock companies across the States and Canada.

Then came World War I and he enlisted in the Navy, but the armistice was declared before he could be sent to any combat zones. He was soon back on the boards and in due course reached New York where he played in *The Hawk*. Four more plays followed and then in 1919 he was on stage in Los Angeles. Here he adopted the name of Richard Dix and made a film test which resulted in his being cast as a villain in a film entitled *One of the Finest* (1919). When he saw how he shaped up in the unsavoury role, he shuddered and forsook the film world.

Two years passed before he decided to give the screen another chance. He played twins in *Not Guilty* (1921) and showed so much promise that the wily entrepreneur Sam Goldwyn signed him to a contract.

In 1923 he took the lead in his first Western, *To the Last Man* (1923), based on a Zane Grey novel inspired by a savage family feud which had taken place in Arizona's 'dark and bloody ground.' Paramount were the producers of this and Dix's *The Ten Commandments* (1923) directed by the dictatorial Cecil B. DeMille. Then it was back to two more Zane Grey Westerns, *Call of the Canyon* (1923) and *The Vanishing American* in which he played Nophaie, a Navajo Indian who, returning home from the Great War, finds his people being exploited by a crooked Indian agent. Nophaie takes to the vengeance trail, at the end of which he dies after learning that thanks to his efforts the Indian agent has been booted out of his job.

The film was brave in its effort to show cinema audiences how the Indians were still being pushed around and hounded by unscrupulous authorities and it was hailed as a masterpiece. Richard's excellent characterization of Nophaie did not, however, earn for him the critical praise he had hoped for, largely because of the oversentimentality of the story. Nevertheless, *The Vanishing American* was a huge success.

Four years later Paramount gave Richard Dix another chance to play a Navajo Indian. The film was *Redskin* (1929) and, script-wise, was better than *The Vanishing American*. Paramount were delighted with the box-office returns. Even so, they did not renew Dix's contract and he was at once snapped up by RKO Radio who, after three movies, handed to him in 1931 the plum role of Yancey Cravat in the

*Opposite: Of all Richard Dix's Westerns – and he made eighteen – *Cimarron* produced in 1931 was doubtless the finest (RKO).*

Right: Richard Dix as General Sam Houston in Man of Conquest, *made in 1939. Here he is, flanked by Max Terhune on the left, and that old faithful, Gabby Hayes (Republic).*

*Tombstone – the Town Too Tough to Die *is notorious for the gunfight in the O.K. Corral. In this scene Victor Jory as Ike Clanton and Edgar Buchanan as Curly Bill Brocius are held at bay by a moustachioed Richard Dix as Wyatt Earp. (Harry Sherman production/Paramount). The film was made in 1942.*

early sound film of Edna Ferber's best-selling novel *Cimarron*. The part of Cravat, the poetic flamboyant adventurer who travels with his wife and young son from the peace of their home in Kansas to the chaos of the lawless town of Sage, Oklahoma, during the land-rush days was tailor-made for Richard.

Although he starred in many profitable pictures after *Cimarron*, that was the peak of his career. He was later cast as General Sam Houston, the avenger of the Alamo disaster, the redoubtable gunman, Wild Bill Hickok and Wyatt Earp, the hero of the O.K. Corral fracas. The three films were *Man of Conquest* (1939), *Badlands of Dakota* (1941) and *Tombstone, the Town Too Tough to Die* (1942).

His last Western was *The Kansan*, (1943). He was playing in a television series called *The Whistler* in 1949 when he collapsed with a heart attack and died on 20 September.

He had been married twice, to Virginia Coe in 1931 and then to Virginia Webster, by whom he had two sons and two daughters.

Richard Dix left behind him an enduring memory of a typical strong, silent he-man, quietly spoken and courteous. In his interpretations he did much to raise the social level of the man of the West. Few boots and saddles stars have equalled his charm and personal kindness. He did his best to further the fortunes of such stars as Ramon Novarro, Irene Dunne and Jeanette MacDonald by recommendations to producers and directors. By common vote, he was 'a good guy'.

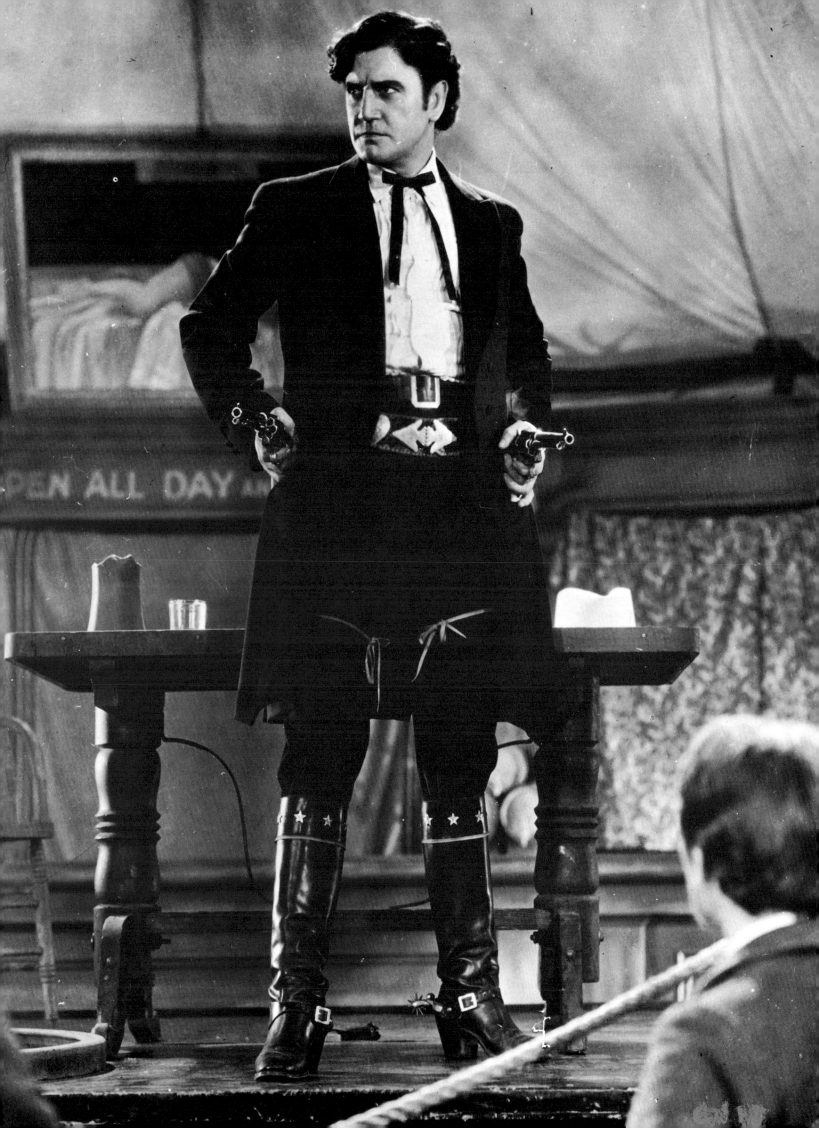

Iron Horse, Iron Man: George O'Brien

Opposite: For his mighty epic The Iron Horse *John Ford chose an unknown to play the hero. The young man seized the opportunity in his powerful fists and immediately soared to stardom. His name – George O'Brien.*

Below: Celebrations were in order when the United States was finally spanned by railroad tracks. This is how John Ford immortalized on film the historic event in The Iron Horse *in 1942 (Fox Film Corporation).*

When Tom Mix went to San Francisco in 1922 to make some personal appearances, the chief of the San Francisco police who controlled the crowds which followed him, was Daniel O'Brien, who made himself personally responsible for the famous cowboy's welfare.

During the visit, Dan O'Brien introduced his son, George, to Tom. George was twenty-two, born on 19 April 1900, a splendid figure of a man and almost too handsome for words. He had served in the US Navy during the Great War and had won the lightweight boxing championship of the Pacific Fleet. He told Tom that when studying at the Polytechnic High School he had been interested in the school dramatic society and rather fancied the acting profession. Tom, grateful for the way Dan O'Brien had taken care of

him, promised to find George a job with his producers, Fox Pictures.

Tom was as good as his word and George was soon an assistant cameraman on the Fox lot. It was at this time that William Fox, more than impressed by the sensational success of *The Covered Wagon*, decided to equal its colossal expense and the grandeur of its conception by producing a film based on the building of the Central Pacific and Union Pacific railroads which on their completion in 1869 spanned the continent from east to west.

To raise the money Fox mortgaged everything he owned, even to his studio and the land on which it stood. He appointed John Ford to direct and hired 5,000 extras, 3,000 horses and 10,000 head of cattle and arranged for several hundred

buffaloes to be rounded up.

Madge Bellamy, a lovely actress, once billed as 'The Most Beautiful Girl on Broadway', was contracted to play the heroine. But neither Fox nor John Ford had yet found the film's hero, though John tested more than fifty actors for the part. Then he noticed a young fellow lugging a camera around for George Schneidermann, one of Ford's favourite lensmen who were to work on *The Iron Horse* (1924).

The assistant cameraman, in his mid-twenties, was of heroic proportions. With a chest measurement of forty-four inches, tall and muscular, he admirably fitted the image of a tough, resolute Western adventurer, an iron man to match the Iron Horse. He was a good horseman and a first-class stuntman who had already played bit parts in two or three movies. But how well could he act? Two tests and John Ford had found in George O'Brien his man.

The Iron Horse was an out-door epic and an all-time winner.

It was a heady success for George

Gun to gun, a typical Western stand-off. 'So who shoots first?' George O'Brien wants to know in this still from Fair Warning, *a 1930 film (Fox Film Corporation).*

O'Brien who had become a close friend of John Ford during production. George earned the critics' applause for this, the first of ten John Ford films in which he was to star.

With this one smash hit, George shot to the top of Fox's list of contract players and, billed country-wide as 'A Man's Man and an Idol of Women', began a long series of films for Fox that was to last for twelve years.

Two years after *The Iron Horse*, he starred in two Westerns, *Rustlin' for Cupid* (1926) and *Three Bad Men* (1926), the latter another of John Ford's master-pieces. George's star was now really in the ascendant.

It was a time when European directors were flocking to Hollywood, men like Ernst Lubitsch, Alexander Korda, Erich Von Stroheim and Friedrich Murnau, who was anxious to make a typical German-type movie, earthy and sexy, entitled *Sunrise* (1927).

The story concerned a young oaf of a farmer seduced by an alluring vamp from the big city. He is so beguiled by her sophisticated charms that he listens willingly when she tries to entice him into drowning his wife and then cunningly contriving to make the murder appear an accident. After a storm of inner torment, he rejects her and makes peace with his wife while the nubile sex-pot returns to life in the city.

To take the lithe, swift-thinking hero of *Three Bad Men* and turn him into the clumsy fumbling farmer of *Sunrise* took some doing, but between them George O'Brien and Friedrich Murnau managed it and George's acting career reached its zenith. He was hailed as one of the brightest stars in Hollywood's spangled heavens.

Fox tried to capitalize on their leading man's popularity by starring him in a part-Biblical, part modern feature, *Noah's Ark* (1928) but thereafter he never made the really big time again. All the same, good actor as he was, he could scarcely fail to retain his stellar status. He started to score again when he was offered the part of Buck Duane, badman and Texas Ranger, the he-man gunman of Zane Grey's novel *The Lone Star Ranger*.

The first half of Grey's action-packed book was devoted to the outlaw years of Buck Duane, the second half to his re-

formation and adventures as a Texas Ranger. Somebody at Fox had the bright idea of spinning the yarn out to make two films, *The Lone Star Ranger* and *The Last of the Duanes*, both released in 1930. The role of Buck Duane was calculatingly written to fit George down to the ground, and the films were two of the best Westerns he made – and he appeared in nearly fifty, twenty-six of them either produced or released by Fox.

In 1931, George was featured in the film of another Zane Grey novel, *Riders of the Purple Sage*, which had been filmed six years earlier by Tom Mix. A box-office winner then, the studios reckoned that a talkie version might enjoy a similar very profitable run. It did. Backed by a better script than the Mix film and some truly superb photography of the great outdoors (George's old boss Schneidermann was the cameraman), the film was a sure-fire success. A beautiful actress, Marguerite Churchill, played opposite George. They

Above: George O'Brien had learned the art of pugilism when as a boy he joined the Columbia Park Boys' Club in San Francisco. This is an incident from Arizona Legion, *one of his six 1939 successes for RKO.*

Left: When George O'Brien played The Lone Star Ranger – *yet another Zane Grey classic – in 1930 Sue Carol, perhaps better known in later years as the astute agent and wife of Alan Ladd, was his co-star (Fox Film Corporation).*

fell in love and married in 1933. Two children were born of the marriage and the family settled down happily on the O'Brien ranch in the Malibu Mountains.

Much publicity was always given to his carrying out his own stunts in his pictures and, almost inevitably, in every film he was afforded the opportunity of stripping off his shirt to reveal his rippling muscles and massive chest. How the feminine fans giggled and sighed. George 'Chest' O'Brien he was called and he was the Western hero *par excellence* as he rode through his movies, his sombrero cocked over one eye, coming to the rescue of maidens in distress.

From Fox he moved to RKO Radio and was still making Westerns for them in 1940 when the Nazi armies were over-running Europe. O'Brien rejoined the Navy and was in Pearl Harbor when the Japanese attacked the base on 7 December

1941. He served throughout the War, in the Philippines, the Pacific, the Aleutians and Alaska and when it was all over he had been awarded several campaign medals and battle stars.

In 1948 he was back with RKO to appear with John Wayne and Henry Fonda in John Ford's *Fort Apache* (1948). In it he plays the part of Captain Sam Collingwood who, because of some minor dereliction of duty, has been posted to the small military post of Fort Apache in Arizona. Loyal to the flag, he follows his commanding officer, Lieutenant Colonel Owen Thursday, to death at the hands of the runaway chief Cochise and his Apache warriors, this even though Thursday has always treated him with contempt.

His acting was quite a *tour de force* and with equal success he was to support John Wayne again in Ford's second cavalry film *She Wore a Yellow Ribbon* (1949). Again

Opposite: George O'Brien hugs Marguerite Churchill to him as though he really owns her, and indeed, two years after his Riders of the Purple Sage *was filmed, he married her, in 1933 (Fox Film Corporation).*

Below: With quiet assurance, George O'Brien (far right) held his own against the masterful presence of John Wayne in She Wore a Yellow Ribbon, *John Ford's 1949 blockbuster. From left to right, between Wayne and O'Brien, are Harry Carey Jr., Ben Johnson and John Agar (Argosy Pictures).*

an officer, Major Mac Allshard, George is the commanding officer of hard-bitten Captain Nathan Brittles (John Wayne), due for retirement after long years of unrewarding action in the Indian Wars. Allshard in George's hands is almost a carbon copy of Captain Collingwood, experienced Indian fighter, understanding and sympathetic.

Filmed like *Fort Apache* in Monument Valley, Utah but this time in resplendent Technicolor, the movie was yet another of Ford's 'greats', with parts for many of his 'family' of actors, not only George and John Wayne but Ben Johnson, Victor McLaglen, Harry Carey Jr, Joanne Drew and last but not least, John's brother Francis.

Before Ford had time to cast George in another Western, the Korean War had broken out and George was off from the Indian wars of the movie world to the bloody action of a real war, one of the most nightmarish in American history. He was to remain a commissioned officer for the next thirteen years, not only in the firing line during the Korean War but also later as a naval attache attending NATO conferences in Italy, Britain, Greece, France and Turkey.

His last film, under the direction of his old friend John Ford once again, was *Cheyenne Autumn* (1964). As Major Braden, something of a martinet, George, not so sympathetic as usual, seemed a trifle uneasy in the role. Notwithstanding, he gave his usual excellent performance.

If it was autumn for the Cheyennes, it was also autumn for George O'Brien. His marriage had sadly ended in divorce when he decided to leave his family and his ranch for more service with the Navy in 1951. The years of separation had taken their toll of marital happiness.

Antagonism simmers between Henry Fonda as Lt. Col. Owen Thursday and John Wayne as Capt. Kirby York in the John Ford 1948 movie Fort Apache. *Between them, George O'Brien as Capt. Sam Collingwood watches Thursday with definite misgiving – with just cause, for later in the film Thursday leads his command, including Collingwood, to massacre at the hands of Apaches (Argosy Pictures).*

Days of Glory

These ten years were golden times for Westerns. Sound had added a new dimension to the screen and fans could now listen, fascinated, to the recorded voices of their favourites, the thunder of horses' hoofs and the crash of gunfire. William (Bill) Boyd, Gary Cooper, Randolph Scott, Joel McCrea and John Wayne all galloped to the reverberations of specially orchestrated background music, and Gene Autry, Roy Rogers and Tex Ritter sang their way to fame.

Alias Hopalong Cassidy: William Boyd

Boyd was born on 5 June 1898 in Ohio, the son of a poor labourer. The family, which included four other children besides Bill, moved to Tulsa, Oklahoma in 1902. It was an unlucky move because five years later the father was killed in a mining accident.

Bill was at school, still only nine years old, but he had no alternative but to leave his studies and find work to keep the rest of the family. He took what jobs came along – grocery assistant, surveyor and tool dresser in the oil fields, a lumberjack in Arizona and an orange-picker in California. He became an auto salesman and chauffeur to a wealthy heiress, Diana Ruth Miller.

Of a good height, broad of shoulder and lean in the waist, exceptionally hand-

Harry 'Pop' Sherman had rescued William Boyd from an alcoholic exile three years previously when Boyd starred in this 1938 Hopalong Cassidy oater Heart of Arizona. *In this still he is flanked by oldster Gabby Hayes and Russell Hayden. That's Billy King up on the driving seat (Harry Sherman Productions/Paramount).*

some with very fair wavy hair and a pair of sky-blue eyes, he figured he was cut out for a movie hero and made a round of the studios, taking work as an extra. Cecil B. DeMille spotted him, put his name in his notebook and remembered him later when he wanted a lead for a costume film, *The Road to Yesterday* (1925).

Well satisfied with Bill Boyd's performance as a 17th-century cavalier, DeMille starred him in a magnificently mounted block-buster, *The Volga Boatman* (1926). From then on he had a moderately successful run in films, never quite making the really big time but gaining three wives and a considerable fortune across the decade of the Twenties.

His first wife was none other than the heiress Diana Ruth Miller. When he married her in 1921 he was already playing bit parts for DeMille. They were divorced three years later and he married film actress Elinor Fair who had played op-

posite him in *The Volga Boatman*. This marriage lasted for five years, ending in divorce in 1930, in which year Bill took Dorothy Sebastian, another film actress, for his third wife.

He was now in receipt of a star status salary and owned a magnificent house in Beverly Hills, a beach house at Malibu and a ranch.

Then one day in 1931, police raided a riotous beach party attended by a Broadway actor also named William Boyd and this Boyd was charged with possession of illegal whisky (they were the days of prohibition) and gambling equipment. To the newspaper picture editors the name William Boyd meant only one man, the famous film star. His photographs were hauled out of the files and erroneously printed as those of the arrested man.

Recantations were later published but the damage was done and Bill's popularity plunged. By 1935 he was living on his

Opposite: William Boyd, a one-time big star in Cecil B. DeMille films, gained Western fame in the ever-popular Hopalong Cassidy series, based on the best-selling novels by Clarence E. Mulford.

Below: Cassidy of Bar 20. It was Harry 'Pop' Sherman who contracted to purchase the Hopalong Cassidy rights from author Mulford. The contract was written on toilet paper and lost by Pop during the long train journey back from New York to Hollywood (Harry Sherman Productions/Paramount 1938).

Adolph Zukor presents

CLARENCE E. MULFORD'S "CASSIDY OF BAR 20"

FEATURING WILLIAM BOYD

FRANK DARIEN
RUSSELL HAYDEN
· NORA LANE ·
ROBERT FISKE
JOHN ELLIOTT

A HARRY SHERMAN Production
A Paramount Picture

Directed by Lesley Selander   Screen Play by Norman Houston

wife's acting earnings, and was drinking heavily. One morning he was sleeping off a two-day drunk on the beach at the rear of his house in Malibu when a go-ahead producer, Harry 'Pop' Sherman, knocked on the door.

Pop had conceived the idea of making a film series out of Clarence E. Mulford's famous Bar 20 novels, and had agreed a contract with him. Not over-blessed with funds, Pop approached a couple of second rank actors to play the part of Hopalong Cassidy, James Gleason, a grizzled smart-talking veteran who wanted too much money and David Niven who just roared with laughter. Now Pop Sherman had come to Bill Boyd.

Bill rallied, gave Pop his solemn word that he would quit drinking (and he did) and then sat down to study the part of Hopalong Cassidy. He decided that instead of Mulford's Cassidy, who was a gambling, drinking, smoking, cussing cowpoke never averse to downing his man for keeps, Boyd's Hopalong would be a paragon of virtue.

As Bill pointed out to Pop Sherman, 'Hoppy will always give the badman time to draw first. He will always be neatly dressed in black. Yeah – I know, Western villains always wear black but I'll make a concession if you like. I'll ride a white horse. And let's cut out all Hoppy's Bar 20 crew and settle for a couple of loyal pards, a youngster for the love stuff and a comic old walrus – and who better than Gabby Hayes for that part?'

The first Cassidy film was *Hop-A-Long Cassidy* (1935), later reissued as *Hopalong Cassidy*. James Ellison was Hoppy's young side-kick and George 'Gabby' Hayes the funny man. In his time Gabby played alongside John Wayne, Randolph Scott, Richard Dix, Roy Rogers and Gene Autry. Few people today are aware that, a New Yorker by birth, Gabby Hayes detested acting in Westerns.

In all sixty-six Hoppy films were made before the series ended in 1948. Pop Sherman was responsible for the first fifty-four, and Bill produced the last

twelve. Bill played in them all while Jimmy Ellison gave way to Russell Hayden, Brad King, Jay Kirby, Jimmy Rogers and Rand Brooks. Gabby Hayes was followed in turn by Britt Wood and Andy Clyde.

By 1948 television was all the rage and Bill realized the potential that existed in his Hoppy films. He decided to buy the TV rights to the series and scraped together a third of a million dollars. He was laughed at. The films had been well distributed and exhibited throughout the land. Who'd want to watch these old sagebrush pot-boilers again? The NBC network knew the answer. They ran the films on Saturday mornings for the youngest viewers and Bill Boyd as Hopalong Cassidy became one of the greatest childhood heroes of all time.

Toy guns and outfits, games, sweets, newspaper strips, comic books, radio programmes, records – Hopalong Cassidy Enterprises, founded by Bill, took the world by storm.

Bill retired in 1953 and moved to Palm Desert, California, where he lived happily with Grace Bradley, his fourth wife, whom he had married in 1937, until his death on 12 September 1972.

'When You Call Me That, Smile!': Gary Cooper

Gary (real name Frank) Cooper, the son of English parents, was a true Westerner who was born in Helena, Montana on 7 May 1901. His father, Charles H. Cooper, a rancher and a Montana Supreme Court Justice, had come as a young man from Birmingham and his mother, Alice, from Kent.

Unimpressed with the standard of schooling in Montana in the early years of the century, Cooper Sr. sent Frank and his brother Arthur to a public school in England, there to absorb the culture and graces not available in the Wild West.

After three years Frank was back, having been expelled for fighting. Now fourteen, he was delighted that he would not be returning to the stuffiness of an English school and could revel in life on his father's ranch, helping the cowhands brand the cattle, learn to shoot and ride and sleep summer nights away under the stars at round-up time.

Schooling was not yet at an end and he was enrolled in a local school, there to lose his English accent and acquire the lazy drawl on which he was later to capitalize so profitably.

He was twenty-three, with school and college days behind him, when his parents moved temporarily to California. Frank, professing a modicum of drawing talent, elected to remain behind in Helena to try his luck at earning a living freelancing as a newspaper cartoonist. His ideas were pretty good, his drawing left something to be desired.

Disappointed at his lack of success, Frank decided to leave Helena and join his parents in Los Angeles, whose newspaper editors appreciated Frank's ability as a cartoonist even less than those back home and Frank soon found himself at a loose end. Then he met up with a couple of cowpuncher buddies from Helena who were now film extras and it did not take Frank long to learn that he too could pick up a few bucks riding with the posses that were going thataway on the Hollywood backlots.

He was now six feet three in height, of a rustic grace and a retiring demeanour that belied the hidden drive. Lean and handsome, of a friendly disposition, good stuntman and splendid horseman, he was soon singled out for something better than tumbling from his saddle at a headlong gallop, doubling for some celluloid hero who didn't know a hackamore from a cinch.

Like all aspiring actors, Frank now looked round for an agent and was recommended to Nan Collins, well-known in Hollywood. There was another Frank Cooper acting in films, so she suggested

Above: Sheriff James Marcus and Gary Cooper in a confrontation in The Texan, *filmed in 1930 (Paramount).*

Opposite: Gary Cooper learned to ride as a youngster on his father's ranch in Montana. Here he is in The Westerner, *which he made in 1940 for United Artists.*

Below: Gary Cooper and Merle Oberon starred in The Cowboy and the Lady *in 1938 (Samuel Goldwyn Productions).*

that her new protégé should change his name, and chose Gary from her home town of Gary, Indiana.

Then she found him small parts in eight or nine movies before a real chance came along, a small role in *The Winning of Barbara Worth* (1926) for United Artists. He did well and Paramount thought him good enough to play the lead a few months later in two more Westerns, *Arizona Bound* (1927) and *Nevada* (1927).

Two years later he was a contract player with Paramount when that studio decided to produce a new Western. It was a re-make of *The Virginian* (1929), based on Owen Wister's book. It had already been filmed three times, in 1902, 1918 and 1925 and it was to be a Joel McCrea

vehicle in 1946. But it will always be Gary Cooper's *Virginian*.

A master of the terse phrase, Gary won immortality when the crook Trampas facing him across a poker table and losing patience with the Virginian's dilatory play, bursts out 'Your bet, you son of a b – .' The word dies on his lips as the Virginian places his gun on the table and murmurs 'When you call me that, *smile!*' It is one of Filmland's best quotes.

The Virginian was a hit, and so was Gary Cooper. From now on he was a top star, at one period earning a higher salary than any other actor in Hollywood.

Top actresses clamoured to play opposite him. Their names read like a Hollywood Parade of the most famous film actresses of all time: Marlene Dietrich, Carole Lombard, Claudette Colbert, Joan Crawford, Jean Arthur, Merle Oberon, Susan Hayward, Barbara Stanwyck, Ingrid Bergman, Paulette Goddard, Patricia Neal, Grace Kelly, Audrey Hepburn, Rita Hayworth and Deborah Kerr. His films were by no means all Westerns but it is for the movies that his presence transformed into Western classics that he is probably best remembered. Apart from *The Virginian* there were *Fighting Caravans* (1931), *The Plainsman* (1936), in which he played a memorable Wild Bill Hickok and, of course, the immortal *High Noon* (1952), directed by Fred Zinneman. In this, his portrayal of the sheriff, deserted by his friends and fellow-townsmen and standing alone against four cold-blooded killers, is Gary Cooper at his best. The part seems so much his that it is surprising to learn that he was offered it because it had been turned down by Gregory Peck who thought that the role of Sheriff Will Kane was too similar to the lone gunman he had played in *The Gunfighter* (1950).

In 1933 Gary married Sandra Shaw, real name Veronica Balfe, and an aspiring film actress. From their first meeting at a party given by her uncle, the famous art director Cedric Gibbons, it had been love at first sight. Their only child, a daughter named Maria, was born on 15 September 1937.

For 23 more years Gary Cooper was to grace the silver screen, one of the all-time greats. His last film was a whodunnit, *The Naked Edge*, that he made at the end of 1960 in England. Cancer had him already

GARY COOPER
MERLE OBERON
THE
Cowboy
AND
the Lady

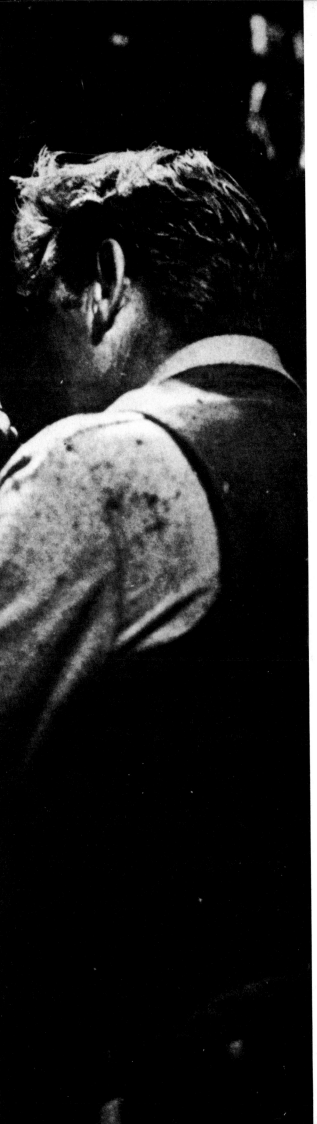

in its grip when, filming completed, he returned to Hollywood where he died peacefully on 14 May 1961.

During his lifetime Gary Cooper was honoured three times by the Academy of Motion Pictures and Sciences. In 1941 he was awarded the Oscar for Best Actor of the Year for his performance in *Sergeant York* (1941) based on the true story of America's greatest hero of World War One. He received a similar award in 1952 for his Sheriff Will Kane in *High Noon*. His third and last was an honorary Oscar for services to the industry in 1960.

He was too ill to attend the ceremony and receive his last Oscar, and his old friend James Stewart received it for him. The world at large realized that night that a certain man from Montana would never unlimber his six-gun on the screen again.

Opposite: A sheriff is entitled to dauntless support on the part of his deputy when the chips are down. Gary Cooper aims to prove this to his faltering deputy Lloyd Bridges in High Noon, *a 1952 triumph (Stanley Kramer Productions).*

Below: An odd turn of events compels Gary Cooper, the taciturn hero, to join forces with Burt Lancaster, the grinning killing outlaw, over a Gatling gun in Vera Cruz, *a boisterous film of double-dealing south of the Border, produced in 1954 (Hecht-Lancaster).*

83

The Lone Gun: Randolph Scott

George Randolph Scott, or Randy as he has always been called by his friends, first saw light of day on 23 January 1903. His father, a Virginian, was George C. Scott, a well-to-do engineer employed by a textile company, who always wanted the boy to become an engineer too, but Randy, having graduated from the University of North Carolina, told his father that he wanted to be an actor. George Scott and his wife Alice did not attempt to smother their son's aspirations; instead they advised him to try Hollywood.

In 1932 Randy was learning his trade with a repertory group at the Pasadena Community Playhouse, and was noticed by a talent scout from Paramount.

The usual film test followed and Randy's performance met with approval. The studio cautiously tried him out in a couple of quickies and then gave him his chance to play with Cary Grant and Nancy Carrol in *Hot Saturday* (1932). He and Cary became firm friends during shooting and still are.

Randy held his own in the film, which was well received. A few months later he was riding the range for the first time in *Heritage of the Desert* (1933), based on a Zane Grey novel. Again Randy acquitted himself capably and was soon back in the saddle again for Zane Grey's *Wild Horse Mesa* (1933).

Both films, which signalled the advent of director Henry Hathaway, later to become famous for his Westerns, were box office winners. The combination of Hathaway/Scott/Grey proved so financially successful for Paramount that during the next twelve months *Man of the Forest*, *To The Last Man* (Shirley Temple's first film), *Sunset Pass* and *The Thundering Herd* (all 1933) went before the camera. Harry Carey rode alongside Randy in the first and last of these four.

With so many Randolph Scott pictures to release, Paramount slowed the merry-go-round and Randy took his time over *The Last Round-Up* and *Wagon Wheels*, a remake of Gary Cooper's *Fighting Caravans*, both Westerns and his only films for 1934. Randy was becoming known as a reliable sagebrush star. Not for another fourteen years, however, did he settle for Westerns exclusively.

A big social event of March 1936 was Randolph Scott's marriage to Marianna Du Pont Somerville, ex-wife of millionaire sportsman, Tommy Somerville. Marianna was a rich woman in her own right and socially she and her new husband were well paired but on a personal level they were not and the marriage only lasted two years.

When the US entered World War II in 1941, Randy had behind him some excellent Westerns, among them *The Last of the Mohicans* (1936), *Jesse James* (1939), *Frontier Marshal* (1939) *Virginia City* (1940) with Humphrey Bogart and *Western Union* (1941).

Due to an old back injury he was considered unfit for war service, but compensated with a series of first-class war films.

In March 1944 he married for the second time. His new wife was Marie Stillman and two children were born of their happy marriage.

After the war, it was saddle and spurs again for *Abilene Town* (1946), which was a hit. Two more bulls-eyes were scored with *Badman's Territory* (1946) and *Trail Street* (1947).

Never again was Randy Scott to star in anything but a Western. One after another

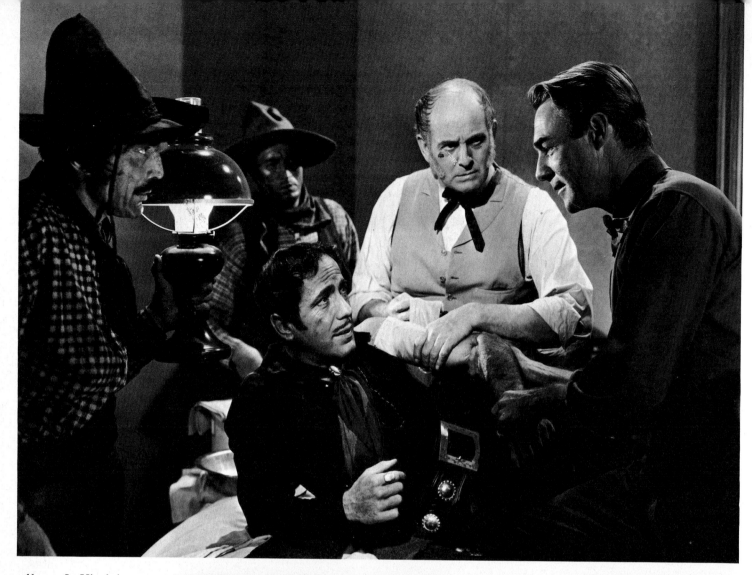

Above: In Virginia City, *1940, Randy Scott played a Confederate officer endeavouring to transport shipments of gold to the beleaguered armies of Robert E. Lee. Errol Flynn opposes him and wins out, but one would have expected that, if only for the fact that Randy's untrustworthy lieutenant was Humphrey Bogart as a Mexican bandit (Warner).*

Right: It was in Abilene Town *in 1946 that Randy Scott listened attentively to Edgar Buchanan explaining how to cheat honestly at cards (Jules Levey Productions).*

they hit the screen: *Return of the Badmen*
(1948), *Canadian Pacific* (1949), *Colt .45*
(1950), *The Bounty Hunter* (1954) and
twenty-two others, down to *Seven Men
from Now* (1956).

The latter was a milestone in Randy's
career for it marked his first association
with director Budd Boetticher. Before
Seven Men from Now, Randolph Scott had
won much praise as a cowboy star. His
performances were better than run-of-the-
mill but not good enough to rank him
amongst the 'Best of the West'. Under
Boetticher's direction, he acquired that
eminence. Together they made six first-
class Westerns apart from *Seven Men from
Now*: *The Tall T* (1957), *Decision at
Sundown* (1957), *Buchanan Rides Alone*
(1958), *Ride Lonesome* (1959), *Westbound*
(1959) and *Comanche Station* (1960), none
of them running for more than seventy-
seven minutes.

It was quite an accomplishment, for
Randy was 53 when *Seven Men from Now*
was made and 57 when *Comanche Station*,
his last with Boetticher was completed.
Then he retired for three years, returning
with his old friend Joel McCrea for one
last great Western, *Ride the High Country*
(1962), under the brilliant direction of the
superb Sam Peckinpah.

In 1971 Randy underwent surgery at
the Mayo Clinic in Rochester, Minnesota,
to correct a hernia and since then has been
enjoying a well-earned retirement, one of
the richest of film stars, the owner of much
property in Palm Springs and the San
Fernando Valley.

Local Boy Makes Good: Joel McCrea

Joel McCrea was a local boy, born on 5 November 1905 in Los Angeles, and was educated at the Hollywood High School. From there he entered the University of Southern California and later moved to Pomona College. Away from school he had found part-time work as a ranch-hand and also as a newspaper delivery boy. One of his customers on his delivery route was none other than that sphinx-like star, William S. Hart. Naturally Joel was an avid fan of the actor and dreamed that one day he might act in Westerns himself. To this end, he took up acting while still at Pomona College and then, to gain professional acting experience, joined the Pomona Community Playhouse.

Film extra work for a tall, handsome youth with some acting and much riding experience was not so difficult to find in the 20s and if he was also prepared to risk life and limb doubling for the stars, he would be welcomed.

He seemed all set for sagebrush derring-do but when he was picked for a feature role it was in *The Jazz Age* (1929). Then an old school friend, Cecil B. DeMille's daughter Cecilia, may have helped secure him a small part in DeMille's first talkie *Dynamite* (1929).

In 1930, Joel McCrea was given his first chance at stardom in an action Western *The Silver Horde*. It was not a great film but in it Joel won his spurs. Moreover, he was moving in Tinseltown's lush social circle, dating such charmers as Constance Bennett and an actress with whom he was later to make some top-notch Westerns, Barbara Stanwyck.

During the 1930s Joel appeared in many movies, mostly non-Westerns although perhaps *Barbary Coast* (1935) with its background of early San Francisco's gambling halls might be regarded as a fringe Western.

In 1933 Joel married an up-and-coming young actress, Frances Dee, with whom he co-starred in a somewhat pedestrian Western, *Wells Fargo* (1935). He and Frances, still happily married, have three sons.

Union Pacific with Robert Preston and Barbara Stanwyck was his sole Western contribution in 1939 and it was a success, directed as it was by the man who was now Joel's personal friend, Cecil B. DeMille.

After appearing in Preston Sturges' flop *The Great Moment* (1944) as a pioneering practitioner in anaesthesia, Joel forsook such miscasting for *Buffalo Bill* (1944), a winner for both Joel and his studio, Fox.

Left: In 1939 Cecil B. DeMille set his hand on Union Pacific and called upon Joel McCrea to play the part of a railroad overseer, with interference from Brian Donlevy as an unscrupulous gambler and sundry plundering bands of Indians. The sinister guy seated behind Joel is Anthony Quinn (Cecil B. DeMille/Paramount).

Below: It was 1949 when Joel McCrea and Alexis Smith played opposite each other in South of St. Louis. It was a comparatively run-of-the-mill Western that still contrived to be entertaining. Victor Jory took care of the villainy (United States Pictures).

WARNER BROS.
present
"SOUTH OF ST. LOUIS"
COLOR BY TECHNICOLOR
★
JOEL McCREA
ALEXIS SMITH
ZACHARY SCOTT
DOROTHY MALONE

A UNITED STATES PICTURES PRODUCTION

He was *The Virginian* in the 1946 remake of Owen Wister's classic novel and so successful was he that he decided henceforth to remain in the sagebrush. Every Western he made thereafter, and there were 25 of them, was a high-budget movie and it seemed as though he could never put a foot wrong.

The best of his Westerns was probably *Ride the High Country* (1962) with Randolph Scott, and directed by Sam Peckinpah. After *Cry Blood, Apache* (1970) with his son and *Mustang Country* (1976) Joel hung up his guns.

Wisely, he had made excellent property investments – perhaps he recalled his role in *The Great Man's Lady* (1942) when oil was found on his land – and today is an extremely wealthy man, still riding the range on his own ranch. In his own expressed opinion he was never a star, but his fans will have none of that. To them Joel McCrea was and always will be the proud rider of the high lonesome.

The Duke: John Wayne

His full name was Marion Robert Morrison, later changed to Marion Michael Morrison when his younger brother Robert was born. He was a schoolboy running around with an Airedale terrier he had named Duke when he began calling in at the local fire-station to listen to the thrilling tales recounted by the firefighters. Beside the little fellow the dog stood big, so before long the two were

When John Wayne was filming Rio Grande *for John Ford in 1950 he took his son Pat along (Argosy/Republic Pictures).*

being called Big Duke (the dog) and Little Duke (the boy). To the end of his life Marion Michael Morrison was called Duke.

Duke was born the son of Clyde and Mary Morrison in Winterset, Iowa, on 26 May 1907. Clyde was a druggist who seemed to lack drive. He also lacked good health and his doctor advised him to go to sunny California, where Duke Morrison spent his school days in Glendale, then a rural community outside Los Angeles.

He was at Glendale Union High School in 1925 when he accepted a foot-ball scholarship to the University of South-ern California. Here he was a star player for the University football team, the Trojans. Tom Mix was an ardent fan and at the end of the 1927/28 season suggested to Howard Jones, the Trojans' coach, that in return for all the free seats he had received from Jones, the trainer could send along a couple of his players to work for a few weeks at the Fox studio where Tom was busy making one Western after another. Duke Morrison was one of the players selected by coach Jones and it was while he was shifting furniture on the lot one day that he happened to catch John Ford's eye. The director gave Duke one or two bit parts.

During the next three years Duke returned to the University, and left again, took on any and every job that was going at the Fox Studio, fell in love with Josephine Saenz, the beautiful daughter of the consul of the Dominican Republic, stowed away on a freighter bound for Honolulu when Josephine's father for-bade him the house, was brought back to California, lodged in prison and then, when he was freed, resumed work at the Fox studio.

He was fortunate enough to be offered the lead in a mammoth movie, *The Big Trail* (1930). Director Raoul Walsh, at a loss for the right leading man, had been nudged in Duke's direction by John Ford. For the film Duke Morrison became John Wayne.

The film earned no rave reviews, but no thumbs down, either, and Duke passed the next nine years playing in sundry 'B' films for Fox, Columbia, Warner Bros, Monogram and Republic, mostly in Westerns.

Then came his big chance. For a few years John Ford had been hawking round the studios a script based on a short story by Ernest Haycox, *Stage to Lordsburg*, and in 1939 United Artists gave him the go-ahead. Ford at once contacted Duke to play the starring role of the Ringo Kid in the film, which was to be called *Stagecoach* (1939).

The film was a triumph and so was John (Duke) Wayne.

When *Stagecoach* was released,

Film hero meets the real thing. John Wayne exchanges a joke with Field Marshal Montgomery while Greer Garson obligingly joins in the merriment.

Duke's future as a superstar was assured. His salary leaped from 200 dollars a week to 1,500. Behind him was the hard slog of more than 60 films across ten years; ahead were many epic movies, in his private life adulation and abuse, two divorces, three marriages, seven children and a long battle with cancer before he died forty years later.

Always staunchly patriotic, he would never hear a word said against his country.

He welcomed the chance of making war films during World War II and his big four were *Flying Tigers* (1942), *The Fighting Seabees* (1944), *Back to Bataan* (1945) and *They Were Expendable* (1945). Not that he deserted the Western trails, for during the same period he made *Three Faces West* (1940), *The Spoilers* (1942), *In Old California* (1942) and *In Old Oklahoma* (1943).

If Duke's professional life was successful, his private life was undergoing severe strain. He had been married to Josephine for six years when he made *Stagecoach* and by then the marriage was just one long quarrel. One year after their last child, Melinda, was born, Duke and Josephine parted. Duke had already fallen in love with the woman who was to become his second wife in 1946, Esperanza Baur, a Mexican actress. Esperanze means 'hope' but she was better known, because of her retroussé nose, by her nickname 'Chata' meaning 'pugnose'. No children were born of this venture which was ill-fated from the start, for Chata insisted that her mother live with them, but during the eight years of their marriage Duke made some of his greatest Westerns. There were John Ford's three cavalry masterpieces, *Fort Apache* (1948), *She Wore a Yellow Ribbon* (1949) and *Rio Grande* (1950), as well as the splendid *Red*

Shirley Temple and Henry Fonda in a scene from John Ford's epic 1948 movie Fort Apache. *John Wayne is perhaps assuring his commanding officer that he certainly will not be wearing that flowered sombrero when next on parade. George O'Brien and Anna Lee look on amusedly (Argosy Pictures).*

River, *Three Godfathers* (1948) (also directed by Ford) and *Hondo* (1953) which was filmed in 3–D and produced by Duke, then *The Searchers* (1956). That the last one was one of his own favourites as well as one of his best is evident from the fact that his son by his third marriage was named Ethan after Ethan Edwards, who in the film sets out on a fanatical search for his two young nieces kidnapped by Comanche Indians.

In 1952 Duke, in Peru on a hunting holiday, met Dick Weldy, an airline public relations manager, and his wife Pilar, thirty years Duke's junior. Duke and Pilar fell in love, the already fragile Weldy marriage ended in divorce and Pilar married Duke in November, 1954. They had three children, two daughters, Aissa and Marisa and a son, Ethan.

Films which followed included *Rio Bravo* (1959), *The Horse Soldiers* (1959) and *The Alamo* (1960), the latter a story which Duke had set his heart on filming. It was produced by his own company, Batjac, but failed to gain the hoped-for

Opposite: John Ford and John Wayne back in action in 1950 with Rio Grande. *Maureen O'Hara plays John's wife (Argosy/Republic Pictures).*

Below: John Wayne put everything he'd got into the making of The Alamo *in 1960, but it failed to become an all-time winner (Batjac Productions).*

Right: It's eyeball to eyeball between Lee Marvin and John Wayne while James Stewart intervenes in the hope of staving off the inevitable. Lee Van Cleef stands ready to back up his outlaw buddy in The Man Who Shot Liberty Valance (Willis Goldbeck/ Paramount).

Opposite: In The Sons of Katie Elder, *produced in 1965 soon after John Wayne had undergone his first serious operation, the old warrior is on the vengeance trail again (Hal Wallis Productions).*

Below: Rooster Cogburn *was the logical sequel to John Wayne's* True Grit. *Katherine Hepburn bears the brunt of the Rooster's disdain for feminine whims and ways, but when courage is the order of the day she's right in there shooting with the best of them.* Rooster Cogburn *was a 1975 movie (Universal).*

success and did not recover its financial outlay for several years.

He was to be hard hit again with the reception accorded *The Green Berets* (1968), another Batjac production. His right-wing beliefs and hawkish comments had already earned him much dislike in certain circles, and this filmic attempt to glorify and justify a very unpopular war did not help. The film eventually amassed 15 million dollars for Wayne.

The next year saw Wayne triumph again in the film that won him his first Oscar, *True Grit* (1969). As Rooster Cogburn, a boozy former outlaw and now a bounty-hunting marshal, he was in his element, and when Barbra Streisand presented him with his Oscar, Wayne was in seventh heaven.

He was already a slowly dying man. After an operation for lung cancer in 1964, Duke was able to say 'I've licked the Big C', and, to show the truth of his assertion, go filming only a few months later in Durango, Mexico, arduously taking tumbles in *The Sons of Katie Elder* (1965).

But the Big C was not licked, only lying dormant. In 1976, three years after he and Pilar had separated amicably, when he was filming his last picture *The Shootist* (1976), in which he played a notorious gunman in the grip of cancer, so was Duke. There was another operation for cancer in 1979, but he died on 11 June. Four years previously his great mentor, John Ford, had also died – and somehow Westerns could never be quite the same again.

Three in Harmony:
Gene Autry, Roy Rogers and Tex Ritter

The many critics who derided the singing cowboys of the film world as artificial, saying 'there never were such folks', were wrong. Gene Autry, Roy Rogers, Tex Ritter and company were carrying on a long established tradition, that of the real cowboys who, when the herds were bedded down at night, sang softly to soothe the nervous, always ready-to-stampede longhorns. Not only that, but they were riding, like the 7th Cavalry, to the rescue not of a besieged wagon train but Western movies in general, for not for the first time and not for the last, Westerns were suffering a popularity slump.

Orvon Gene Autry was born in Tioga, Texas on 29 September 1907, the son of a cattle buyer-cum-farmer who migrated from one place to another before finally settling in Ravia, Oklahoma.

Gene left the local community school at the age of seventeen and took a job as a railroad telegrapher in Chelsea, Oklahoma. Music was in the heart of him. He had already sung at prayer meetings and concerts, and now, earning a weekly salary, was able to buy himself a guitar on a 'play now, pay later' basis.

He managed to obtain a singing stint on Tulsa radio, billed as 'Oklahoma's Yodelling Cowboy'. Twelve months later, a scout from Columbia Records visited him with a proposal that he come to New York to record 'That Silver-Haired Daddy of Mine', an effusion that Gene had co-written. It was a best-seller and Columbia signed him to a contract.

Not long after, when he was in

Gene Autry was Shooting High *with* Jane Withers *in 1940. Two years later he was doing just that again, this time in the US Army Air Corps (Twentieth Century-Fox).*

Chicago crooning away on the National Barn Dance radio programme, Nat Levine, who had just concluded a film deal with Ken Maynard, came to see him to ask him to be in the film, *In Old Santa Fé*, to sing a few numbers between Ken's action sequences. Levine was also interested in Lester Burnette who was singing alongside Autry.

Burnette had been with Gene for two years. Better known as 'Smiley' Burnette,

he was later to make movies not only with Gene but also with Roy Rogers. Neither singer needed asking twice to come to Hollywood. The rest, as the saying goes, is history.

Gene was in top form in *In Old Santa Fé* (1934). Then Nat Levine cast him in a serial *The Phantom Empire* (1935), a mishmash of science fiction and Western. Gene, raw actor that he was, was wooden and stilted, though when he sang he sure

Looks like it's whoopee time for everyone but Gene Autry in this scene from Rancho Grande, *one of seven films he sang through in 1940. Sagebrush comic Smiley Burnette regards Gene quizzically (Republic).*

raised the ceiling. In spite of its daft and incredible plot, the serial was a triumph, the second most profitable film serial ever made. It put the sagging market for Westerns back on its feet and started the craze for cowboy singers. Hundreds of musical Westerns were made and Gene was to star in more than ninety of them.

Gene Autry comics and books, parlour games, toy pistols and cowboy outfits for young fans, pin-ups, records, crockery, car-stickers and much more proliferated; it was estimated that Gene's fortune from all this was somewhere in the hundred million dollar bracket. His fan mail ran to 80,000 letters per month.

In 1942 Gene enlisted as a technical sergeant in the US Army Air Corps, spending the war as a pilot, ferrying personnel to India and the Middle East.

Five years later he was mustered out and returned to Hollywood to pick up where he had left off. He set up his own production unit and for the next six years he shared acting honours with his noble steed, Champion, in more than thirty Westerns.

Gene was swift to take advantage of the new medium, television. For CBA-TV he produced a series, *The Gene Autry Show*. This stint, together with nearly 8,000 benefit performances and his annual cavorting with the Gene Autry's World Championship Rodeo in New York and Boston may well have kept him too busy even to count the torrent of dollars that was flooding into his exchequer.

Every Christmas his 'Rudolph the Red-Nosed Reindeer', of which more than 6,000,000 copies have been sold, is still played on the air, and who does not also recall 'Tumbling Tumbleweeds', 'You Are My Sunshine' and 'South of the Border, down Mexico Way'?

Roy Rogers, originally Leonard Slye, was born on 5 November 1912 in Cincinnatti, Ohio. When he left school, he worked for a time in a shoe factory but soon set off to win fame and fortune with his old second-hand guitar.

He endured the usual gruelling business of playing with bands in dance-halls, at hick barn-dances, on the radio, at carnivals and celebratory functions of all kinds. He finally turned up in Roswell, New Mexico, which had been one of Billy the Kid's happy hunting grounds some fifty years earlier. (Did Roy remind himself of this when he played the part of the young outlaw in *Billy the Kid Returns* in 1938?) Here, as Dick Weston the Texas Troubadour, he linked up with a swinging foursome who called themselves The Four Tumbleweeds.

For Len Slye, alias Dick Weston, it was a short step to Hollywood to make a couple of cheapie Westerns before changing his name for the second and last time to Roy Rogers. Columbia, envious of Gene Autry's success over at Republic, had been on the look-out for a comparable star, and found him when a Columbia talent scout heard Dick Weston and the Tumbleweeds and noted the applause from all quarters.

When Gene Autry enlisted, there was no-one to rival Roy's aspiration to No. 1 Movie Cowboy. After all, did he not have, apart from his vocal achievements, a famous mount, Trigger, 'the smartest horse in the movies'?

Roy was also ably supported by two stalwart comic aides, George 'Gabby' Hayes, who was still hating his way through Westerns and Smiley Burnette, Gene's old pardner. Gabby, too, had appeared often with Gene.

Most of the stars of Western musicals – and there were quite a few – had passable or good voices. But Roy Rogers was to go one better than any of his fellow cowboy

Opposite top: In 1946 Roy Rogers called Douglas Dumbrille to account in another song-and-saddle run-of-the-miller, this time Under Nevada Skies *(Republic).*

Opposite bottom: Roy Rogers and Trigger. What a combination! As Leonard Slye, his real name, Dick Weston and Roy Rogers, he figured in 95 Western movies, three more than Gene Autry.

Left: With the coming of sound, many stars of Western films chose to air their vocal talents. Of all of them, Tex Ritter was the only first-class singer and true son of the West – he hailed from Murvaul, Texas. His record of 'High Noon' was a best-seller.

crooners. In 1946, after the death of his first wife, he married Dale Evans who had appeared in many of Roy's films; together, they were a formidable duet.

Roy followed in Gene's marketing footsteps with comic books and all the other toys and juvenile paraphernalia. His records, such as 'Don't fence me in', 'Happy Trails' and 'Hoppy, Gene and Me', sold in countless numbers. A successful fast food franchise and a museum also contributed to a fortune estimated at over $100 million.

One of his last films was *Son of Paleface* (1952) when he played an undercover agent singing and fighting round the antics of Bob Hope and Jane Russell. Fourteen years later he played an old saddle-tramp riding to the aid of a young boy in *Mackintosh and T.J.* (1976). It was his swan-song so far as films were concerned, though he had been appearing in several television series for many years. Recently this writer dropped in on a Roy Roger's restaurant in Washington. Kids are still enjoying Roy Roger's fare.

Gene and Roy between them appeared in nearly two hundred movies, surely a magnificent achievement for two youngsters who started out with only their voices and their beat-up guitars as tradable assets.

Another two-gun troubadour was Tex Ritter. His musical repertoire was devoted more to the traditional ballads of the old frontier, the immortal Stephen Foster's 'Old Susanna' and the like, than the modern Country-and-Western three-to-a-bar, shake-it-and-roll gig-songs.

Woodward Maurice Ritter was born 12 January 1907 in Murvaul, Texas. His family owned a 400-acre farm and it was during his early years on the farm that young Maurice learned the lore of folk music, seated at the feet of a negro farmhand.

His education at a high school was followed by his induction into the University of Texas to study law. It was the time of the Great Depression and from college he went to work in a steel mill. To the romantic soul of the youth that must have been plain hell. With hindsight it seems almost inevitable that he should turn to singing folk songs on radio, in Houston to be exact.

There followed a road tour which eventually brought him to Chicago. His liking for the law prompted him to enrol in Northwestern University. Now, however, he was so deeply into a singing career that his legal tuition only interfered with his musical activities. There was, moreover, the urge to act.

It was in New York City that he was later afforded the opportunity of understudying Franchot Tone on stage in 'Green Grow the Lilacs', the play on which the amazingly successful 'Oklahoma!' was later based. It was during his stint in 'Green Grow the Lilacs' that he was dubbed Tex by other members of the cast.

Although he received favourable notices for his showing in the production – also for his acting in two other plays, 'The Round-Up' and 'Mother Lode', the latter with Melvyn Douglas – he lost interest in the theatre and returned to radio.

From then on he never looked back. To the end of his life he was up there with the best of them on radio and in recording studios. He graced a radio series 'Lone Star Rangers' with his singing and re-telling of true stories of the West. He featured in drama series such as 'Gang Busters' and 'Death Valley Days'.

In the 1930s he was Tex Mason in 'Bobby Benson's Adventures' and its musical sequel 'Songs of the B-Bar-B'. Then followed a three-year run of 'Cowboy Tom's Roundup', a top-rating in children's radio show. He had planned and created the show himself. He was also greatly in demand by various recording companies.

Screen fame, though, was yet to come. It arrived in the person of producer Edward Finney who called on Tex when he was appearing in a dude ranch show in New Jersey. The year was 1936 and Tex took his infectious grin, resonant voice and guitar to the wilds of Hollywood with alacrity.

Song of the Gringo made that same year was his first film. It is with some amusement that one notes that a judge in the film was played by Al Jennings, one of the last Western outlaws, a garrulous left-over whose daring exploits were by no means all that he cracked them up to be. He talked the director into allowing him to show Tex how to draw and shoot a six-gun. Joe Rosa in his excellent book 'The Gunfighter' (University of Oklahoma Press, 1969) quotes a US Army General who knew Jennings personally as saying that the old loud-mouth 'could have qualified as the traditional bad shot who couldn't hit the side of a barn'.

Modest in production though *Song of the Gringo* was, it launched Tex Ritter on to a movie career of sixty more Western films for Grand National, Monogram, Columbia and Universal. Too old for military service, he yet contrived to make eleven bread-winners for Producers Releasing Corporation in 1944 and 1945.

During his years in Hollywood, riding his horse White Flash and partnering such other leading Western stars as Wild Bill Elliott and Johnny Mack Brown, Tex was recording songs for Decca Records and Capitol Records. It was in 1952 that he recorded his big one, 'High Noon', the theme song for the Gary Cooper classic film.

In 1937, 1938 and 1939 he was among the top ten cowboy stars in the *Motion Picture Herald*'s poll. He was back there again in 1945 when he made *Apache Ambush*, his last Western feature.

If his days as a sagebrush hero were over, he was still far from finished with his other show-biz activities. Throughout the 1950s he hosted and sang in several radio series, continued to record for the top recording companies and went on worldwide personal appearances in Wild West shows. This author well remembers seeing him when he galloped his horse into the arena at Harringay Stadium in London, to the accompaniment of gunfire and the rousing strains of 'High Noon' blaring out of the loudspeakers.

Later he became the Nashville president of the National Committee for the Recording Arts and president and vice-president of the Country Music Association. The year 1970 saw him running for the Republican nomination to the US Senate seat from Tennessee. He was defeated and forsook politics. Four years later he visited a friend in the Nashville city jail and while there collapsed with a fatal heart attack. So died this lovable man of many talents on 2 January 1974.

It was while riding Along the Navajo Trail *in 1945 that Roy Rogers happened on a little pow-wow between Bob Noland, Dale Evans, Roy's wife and gravel-voiced Gabby Hayes (Republic).*

The Western Rides Again

After World War II, Hollywood's answer to entertaining a public sated with horror and bloodshed was comedies, musicals, who-dunnits and Westerns. Apart from Gene Autry's and Roy Rogers' efforts, though, the stark realism of wartime news-reels had swept aside the old style of shoot-em-up Westerns with their simple basic plots. Filmgoers insisted on more down-to-earth fare. That suave charmer Errol Flynn was beguiled into trying to maintain the over-glamorous type of Western. His efforts, though excellent in many respects, could not stand up against the grimmer features in which Henry Fonda, Robert Taylor, still fighting his matinee idol image, James Stewart and Robert Mitchum were to appear, while on the distaff side the materialistic Barbara Stanwyck herded the winsome misses out of Westerns forever.

Swash and Buckle: Errol Flynn

Captain Blood, The Charge of the Light Brigade, The Adventures of Robin Hood and The Dawn Patrol were all behind Errol Flynn when in 1939 he buckled on a pair of six-shooters and made his first Western, Dodge City. The first three super-films mentioned above all co-starred the beautiful Olivia de Havilland and were directed by Michael Curtiz. If Warner Bros. expected the same success with Dodge City with Flynn, Havilland and Curtiz once again contributing their talents, they were disappointed. A prosaic script and uninspired characterization ensured that the movie was an Errol Flynn second-rater (Warner Bros.).

Before the War, famous Westerners such as Tom Mix, Hoot Gibson, Buck Jones, Jack Holt, Ken Maynard and Gary Cooper were all men who had known what it was to mix with and ride with real cowboys, but newcomers such as Fonda and his peers were actors with different backgrounds.

Gone now were the tough cowpokes of the early Westerns. Their place was taken by actors, who, if they weren't true Westerners, can today be considered stars of Western films. Errol Leslie Flynn was one of them. He was born in Hobart, Tasmania on 20 June 1909, and had lived the life of a rakehell from an early age, if his autobiography *My Wicked Wicked Ways* is to be believed. Diamond smuggling and slave trading in the testament according to Flynn were among the more respectable pursuits of his mis-spent youth. His first film was a poor effort entitled *In the Wake of the Bounty* in which he played Fletcher Christian.

He later went to England and joined the Northampton Repertory Company. From there he secured bit parts on the London West End stage and somehow managed to land a contract with Warner Bros who then had studios at Teddington.

He was given the lead in *Murder at Monte Carlo* (1935), a picture of no importance to filmgoers but of great importance to Errol for on the strength of his performance he was sent to Hollywood where that same year he was fortunate enough to play *Captain Blood* (1935).

Swashbuckler followed swashbuckler and then came his first Western, *Dodge City* (1939), opposite his favourite actress Olivia De Havilland. It was a stereotyped story but the film was packed with action, including one of the most spectacular saloon brawls in film history.

Not a great actor, Errol Flynn nevertheless projected an innate charm. In all he made eight Westerns, *Dodge City, Virginia City* (1940), *Santa Fé Trail* (1940), with Ronald Reagan as Lieutenant George Armstrong Custer, *They Died with Their Boots On* (1942) with Flynn now as Custer, *San Antonio* (1945), *Silver River* (1948), *Montana* (1950), and his last, *Rocky Mountain* (1950. Not all were as popular or successful as he might have wished but all were passable to good, *They Died with Their Boots On* being probably the best if not particularly historically accurate.

Errol's *affaires de coeur* were myriad.

An appearance in court on a rape charge did nothing to enhance his screen image of old-world courtesy. He was a philanderer incarnate, given to pursuing teenagers. 'I may be too old for them, but they're not too young for me', was his expressed philosophy. He was married three times, firstly in 1935 to Lili Damita, the fiery French actress by whom he had one son, Sean. After their divorce he married Nora Eddington, a cigar store sales-girl, and by the time they separated they had a daughter Deirdre and a son Rory. Then Errol married Patrice Wymore, a popular film actress who appeared with him in *Rocky Mountain*.

Errol died on 14 October 1959, a world weary drug addict, worn out and prematurely aged, a sad relic of the man who had once been described as 'the handsomest man in the world'.

Gangling Grace: Henry Fonda

Although *The Trail of the Lonesome Pine* (1936) in which Henry Fonda starred was the first outdoor Technicolor film, it cannot be regarded as a real honest-to-God Western, though it does have certain Western elements. Fonda's first real Western was *Jesse James* (1939), in which he played Frank James, Jesse's brother. The title role of the gun-crazy bandit went to Tyrone Power who, in truth, was happier with sword in hand.

At the end of the film Jesse was murdered by his cousin Bob Ford (John Carradine) and the way was open to a sequel, for filmgoers would want to know what happened to the more sympathetic brother, Frank. So Henry Fonda did a smart follow-up with *The Return of Frank James* (1940) wherein he gave Bob Ford (Carradine again) his come-uppance.

Henry Fonda was born on 16 May 1905 in Grand Island, Nebraska, the son of a commercial printer. While still at school, he set his sights on writing and art as a career.

Graduating from high school in 1923 he took a job with the Northwestern Bell Telephone Company and studied journalism part-time at the University of Minnesota. Lack of success impelled him to give up his studies two years later (although in his later years he became a very good artist, and his paintings today are avidly collected), and he took on a clerkship with the Retail Credit Company, but he was still dissatisfied with life.

Mrs. Dorothy Brando, who had two daughters and a one-year-old son named Marlon, was a friend of Henry's mother and also one of the founders of the local Omaha Community Playhouse. The current season was about to begin and the company were in search of a 'juvenile', that is a young actor in his late teens or so. Henry was twenty and Mrs. Brando reckoned that was sufficient to recommend him for the job.

Somewhat reluctantly Henry made his way to the theatre and was accepted after a short reading. For the next eight months, from September 1925 to May 1926, he laboured away during the daytime with the credit company and in the evenings at the theatre. Then he was offered the lead in *Merton of the Movies*. His eight months

as a bit player had sharpened Henry's appetite for acting, and he left his clerk's job to devote himself to his new profession.

A few years later, now a successful actor, he was appearing on the Broadway stage in the lead part of *The Farmer Takes a Wife*. The Fox studios bought the film rights to the play, hoping to star either Joel McCrea or Gary Cooper. Neither star was available at the time and with some misgivings Fox offered the lead to Fonda. To the relief and delight of the money-spiders at Fox, the film was a hit.

Then, in 1939 John Ford was scouting around for an actor to play the coveted part of the *Young Mr. Lincoln* (1939), and decided with uncanny instinct to extend the opportunity to Henry. From the start Ford hit it off with Fonda and Hank, as

Opposite: Hank Fonda reloads his six-shooter in Firecreek prior to taking over control of the town from James Stewart who has been left to his fate by the local Citizens. Firecreek is a so-so routiner of 1968 (Warner Bros.).

Below: Henry Fonda's sterling performance as Frank James in Jesse James *with Tyrone Power and Nancy Kelly led to a sequel,* The Return of Frank James. *Both films were box-office successes for Twentieth Century-Fox. They were made respectively in 1939 and 1940.*

Above: Henry Fonda and Claudette Colbert co-starred in this John Ford movie, Drums Along the Mohawk *filmed in 1939 (Darryl F. Zanuck Production/ Twentieth Century-Fox).*

Opposite: Linda Darnell and Henry Fonda in John Ford's My Darling Clementine, *a 1946 hit (Darryl F. Zanuck Production/Twentieth Century-Fox).*

Overleaf: From left to right, standing, are Dick Foran, Pedro Armendariz, Ward Bond, Victor McLaglen and Henry Fonda in Fort Apache *(Argosy Pictures).*

Ford always called him, was promptly enrolled in the Ford school of actors which numbered amongst its ranks John Wayne, Ward Bond, George O'Brien, Jane Darwell, John Carradine.

Young Mr. Lincoln was a triumph not only for Ford but also for Fonda. Later that same year, Hank served the director well again in *Drums Along the Mohawk* (1939). Claudette Colbert played opposite him in this drama of the Revolutionary War. In 1946 Ford starred Hank in the splendid *My Darling Clementine,* Fonda bringing his gangling grace to the part of Wyatt Earp, marshal of Tombstone, the 'town too tough to die'. Two years later Fonda excelled as the doomed Colonel Thursday in *Fort Apache* (1948) with John Wayne.

Henry Fonda was now regarded as one of the great stars of Western films. In later life, a superstar who had appeared in many different types of movies, he was always happy to don his chaparejos and take to the prairie. As he grew too old to play the hero, producers started to cast him against type and he scored a resounding success in the 'spaghetti' Western *Once Upon a Time in the West* (1968) with Jason Robards and Charles Bronson. Hank played a double-dyed villain and the film is nowadays considered a minor classic.

In 1981 Henry Fonda was awarded the Oscar for Best Actor for his part in *On Golden Pond* (1981). It was his last film, for he died on 12 August 1982. He had been married five times and his daughter Jane and son Peter have both become stars in their own right.

Pretty Boy: Robert Taylor

Robert Taylor, tall, dark and handsome, was so famous for his good looks that envious critics labelled him 'Powder puff'.

His appearance with the legendary Greta Garbo in *Camille* (1936), when it was a toss-up as to who was the more beautiful, may have had a lot to do with the derision. But one can blame the studio make-up boys for that, for they excelled themselves even to Taylor's carefully plucked and delicately pencilled eyebrows and lipsticked mouth. That sort of thing had been all right back in the days of Rudolph Valentino but this was the late 1930s.

Taylor changed all that. He insisted on tough roles – he was a boxer in *The Crowd Roars* (1938) and a gangster in *Johnny Eager* (1941) – and when it came to guns-and-saddle he proved very effective. *Stand Up and Fight* (1939) was his first cowboy feature; two years later he donned a black outfit for *Billy the Kid* (1941). He was already thirty-one (he was born in 1911 and quaintly christened Spangler Arlington Brough), ten years older than the real Billy the Kid had been when he was shot dead by Pat Garrett. Even so,

Taylor gave a fine performance as the ruthless gunman with an unexpectedly susceptible heart and so self-sacrificing that when faced by the sheriff, Pat Garrett (played by Brian Donlevy), he deliberately delays his draw so that Garrett can kill him.

Taylor was excellent as an unshaven cavalry scout in his next Western, *Ambush* (1949), based on the novel of the same name by the best-selling author Luke Short. Thereafter, he spurred through thirteen more Westerns, taciturn, usually unsmiling and forbidding except for one light-hearted romp, *Many Rivers to Cross* (1955).

Taylor originally came from Filley, Nebraska, the son of a doctor, and at first fancied himself as a cellist. He forsook music for acting and was spotted by a talent scout when appearing at the Pomona Drama School. He was signed by MGM in 1934 and stayed there for 25 years. He married first Barbara Stanwyck in 1939 and, after their divorce in 1952, film actress Ursula Thiess in 1954.

Cancer claimed him in 1969 after a long and brave fight.

Slow Talker and Fast Gun: James Stewart

Opposite top: Broken Arrow, *1950, was one of James Stewart's big successes. Jeff Chandler is Cochise, war-chief of the Apaches (Twentieth Century-Fox).*

Opposite bottom: How The West Was Won *was a sprawling 1962 movie that included James Stewart (seen here), Gregory Peck, Debbie Reynolds, Walter Brennan and John Wayne. (MGM).*

Below: The only resemblance between Tom Mix's earlier film Destry Rides Again *and this James Stewart/Marlene Dietrich remake of 1939 was the title. (Universal).*

If ever a laconic, drawling, deceptively slow-moving character drifted through one Western after another, it was James Stewart who exemplified type-casting of that kind in most of his films and particularly as the deputy sheriff in *Destry Rides Again* (1939). *Destry* is probably the best-loved of his movies, backed up as he was by Marlene Dietrich throatily chortling 'See what the Boys in the Back Room will have', Brian Donlevy as the slick saloon-keeper and Charles Winninger as the tipsy sheriff.

James Maitland Stewart hails from Indiana, Pennsylvania where he was born on 20 May 1908. At Princeton University he was soon involved in amateur dramatics and his liking for the stage led him to leave the university and take off for several years' hard grind in stock companies.

In 1932, in company with his friend Henry Fonda, he was playing bit parts on the Broadway stage. It was actress (later gossip columnist) Hedda Hopper who recommended him to MGM as an actor of promise. He was tested and given a contract. After a faltering start as a reporter in *The Murder Man* (1935) with Spencer Tracy, he was handed the role of Jeanette MacDonald's brother in *Rose Marie* (1936), capably holding his own against the vocal onslaught of Jeanette and Nelson Eddy.

From then on, James Stewart was headed for stardom, winning an Oscar for Best Actor for his part in *Mr. Smith Goes to Washington* (1939). When war broke out James enlisted in the Army Air Force. He was in action over Germany and during his war service rose to colonel. After the war, he stayed in the Air Force Reserve and in 1961 was promoted to the rank of Brigadier General.

His fifteen Westerns were all high-budget features. Those deserving special mention include two 1950 films *Winches-*

ter '73 and *Broken Arrow* in which he appeared with Jeff Chandler who played the part of Cochise, war-chief of the Chiricahua Apaches. Then, too, everyone who saw *How The West Was Won* (1963) will always remember James Stewart as a pioneer trapper in it. Stewart, like his old friend Hank Fonda, became one of John Ford's happy band and under his direction took part in *Two Rode Together* (1961) *The Man Who Shot Liberty Valance* (1962) and *Cheyenne Autumn* (1964).

Stewart and Fonda acted together in *Firecreek* (1968). It was another villainous role for Fonda, one that did not please him a lot for in it he attempted to shoot Stewart and, as he said, 'Any man who tries to kill Jimmy Stewart has to be written down as a man who's plain rotten. You can't get much lower than that.' The sentiment says much for the likeable fellow that James Stewart has always played and really is.

Sleepy and Sinister: Robert Mitchum

A man of many parts, Robert Mitchum can move from light comedy to cold-blooded slaying and then to heroic deeds with facile ease. As he says, 'I've played everything except women and children'.

He was born on 6 August 1917 in Bridgeport, Connecticut. Four high schools did their best to rouse him from his dreamy languor and pay heed to the principles of the three Rs but to no avail. His first attempt to elude the rigours of education and the vigilance of his parents was to run away from home at the age of six. Brought back in disgrace, he took to his heels again at every opportunity and by the time he was fourteen had already wandered across most of New England.

He was sixteen when he slipped un-

observed on to a train bound for California, but unable to find a job, he returned home and drifted aimlessly from one boring job to another.

He fell in love and married Dorothy Spence of Camden, New Jersey and the happy couple honeymooned in California where Bob's sister Julie was working as an actress with the Long Beach Theatre Guild. Eventually, after various jobs and rejection by the US forces when he tried to enlist, Bob joined the Long Beach Theatre Guild and acted in several plays.

Julie's agent took on Bob as well and hawked his photo and curriculum vitae round the studios. Eventually, in 1943 he told Bob to learn to ride a horse and not shave for a couple of weeks, as Bill Boyd was looking for a baddie to play opposite him in his next Hopalong.

So it came about that Bob's first movie was *Hoppy Serves a Writ* (1943), and he was so villainous that Bill Boyd used him in seven more Hopalong oaters.

If Bob could not join the regular army, he could at least *act* the part of a military man and gave very creditable performances in several war films.

During this period he also made Westerns. *Nevada* (1944) was his first starring vehicle, replacing Tim Holt who had been drafted. Then came *West of the Pecos*

(1945) in which he played the lead again.

A real opportunity to shine came in *The Story of G.I. Joe* (1945), then the US Government decided that hostilities could perhaps be brought to a quicker conclusion if Robert Mitchum, film star, could take an official part in the war proper, and called him up.

Their hopes were fulfilled. No sooner had Bob turned up for active duty than the war ended. After his discharge he must have felt at ease with his part in *Till the End of Time* (1946), when he played a veteran back from the war. After that his

Here again is young Bob Mitchum in his first featured role in Hoppy Serves a Writ *with William Boyd (Paramount).*

Right: In Nevada, *a Robert Mitchum Western of 1944, the erstwhile baddie of* Hoppy Serves a Writ *is now an honest cowpoke combating a bunch of no-goods aiming to take over some mining claims. Young Harry McKim seems anxious to get Bob out there on Main Street and start shootin'* (RKO).

Opposite bottom: Marilyn Monroe played a dance hall singer in River of No Return *in 1954, and very good she was too. Deserted by her no-good gambler husband she turns to Robert Mitchum, a not-too-surprisingly sympathetic widower. Here she is tending his wounds after being mauled by a mountain lion* (Twentieth Century-Fox).

career leaped forward and today he is still up there in front, leading the pack in TV stunners such as *The Winds of War* (1983).

The Night of the Hunter (1955) was probably the best of Mitchum's Westerns. His portrayal of a psychopathic killer is possibly his most compelling in any of his more than 130 motion pictures. This was the only movie directed by Charles Laughton who professed a tremendous admiration for Bob as an actor.

Mention should also be made of *River of No Return* (1954), if only for the fact that Mitchum's co-star was Marilyn Monroe.

In 1959 came *The Wonderful Country* in which Mitchum played a Texan bandit recruited by two Mexican guerilla leaders, Pedro Armendariz and Victor Mendoza, to indulge in a little gun-running for them. In *El Dorado* (1967), Robert Mitchum more than held his own against the towering personality of John Wayne. Bob played a drunken sheriff hauled back onto the teetotal trail by Big John. For *The Good Guys and the Bad Guys* (1969) he happily accepted the role of an ageing sheriff spurned by the mayor when he tries to warn him about the return of an old-time outlaw, played by George Kennedy, bent on revenge. The theme was serious, the screen-play comic, the film a big box-office triumph.

Bob has two sons, both of whom have inherited their father's love of acting.

His great height, his deceptively lazy manner and his shambling gait perhaps belie the fact that he is extremely interested and successful in the arts. He has had short stories and poems published, music written by him performed and children's plays produced. Yes, indeed, Robert Mitchum is a man of many parts.

Above: Marvin Balsam as the mayor of Progress, eyes Sheriff Robert Mitchum from the 1969 movie The Good Guys and the Bad Guys *(Warner Bros.-Seven Arts/Robert Goldstein Productions).*

Tough but Tender: Barbara Stanwyck

Opposite: Annie Oakley, which starred Barbara Stanwyck in 1935, was a fore-runner to the great musical Annie Get Your Gun. *Annie, of course, was Buffalo Bill's little sure-shot, a leading light in the old scout's Wild West Show (RKO).*

Moroni Olsen as Buffalo Bill doffs his sombrero and introduces Barbara Stanwyck to an enthusiastic audience in Annie Oakley *(RKO).*

In 1944 the US Treasury Department named film actress Barbara Stanwyck as America's highest paid woman – not a bad achievement for a lass who had been born to an impoverished family thirty-seven years previously in Brooklyn.

She was the youngest of five children, born Ruby Stevens on 16 July 1907 and still quite young when orphaned. She was only thirteen when she was working as a parcel-wrapper but her eyes were already on the bright lights. An elder sister was a showgirl and helped Ruby to a dancing job in a downtown speakeasy. At that time she was scarcely fifteen and possibly it was at this tender age in those dingy surroundings that she acquired that worldly, wary expression that seemed so much a part of her screen persona.

She danced her way out of the speakeasy and on to the Broadway stage where at nineteen she was leading the cast in the stage version of *Noose*. It was now that she met and married Frank Fay, an extremely handsome light comedy actor. She also adopted the name of Barbara Stanwyck.

Her first film was *Broadway Nights* (1927), a silent movie out of the Warner Bros stable. Three years later she was given fourth billing in *The Locked Door* (1930) in which she was called upon to cavort for most of the time in a ripped dress, coyly displaying a lacy brassiere and cringing under third degree.

The Locked Door was filmed in New York but Hollywood was interested in Frank Fay. Barbara accompanied him to California and to the office of Harry Cohn, the ruthless and detested boss of Columbia, where Frank did his best to explain to Harry what a whizz of an actress his wife was. Harry, in an unusually generous mood, offered Barbara a part in a 'B' film, *Mexicali Rose* (1930).

Harry Cohn must have approved of her acting for a few months later she was taking the lead in Columbia's *Ladies of Leisure*, directed by Frank Capra. Barbara was at her best as a beautiful gold-digger and she was rewarded with a contract.

Successful she might have been, happy in her domestic life she was not. She and Frank Fay had reached the parting of the ways and a divorce was arranged. A son, Dion, had been born of the marriage.

Now in great demand, she made a succession of films before appearing in her first big Western *Annie Oakley* (1935) opposite Preston Foster and Melvyn Douglas.

She was flourishing her six-shooters again in Cecil B. DeMille's *Union Pacific* (1939) to the admiration of Joel McCrea

and Robert Preston. In the same year she married Robert Taylor and lived with him happily for thirteen years until he decided to pull out. She took the resultant divorce very hard.

The Great Man's Lady (1942) was part-Western, once again with sturdy Joel McCrea. The film was inexcusably dull, unworthy of the woman who was now one of Hollywood's reigning queens.

California (1946) was Barbara's next Western. Ray Milland, the English actor, played a wagonmaster with a secret past while Barbara turned in her now-expected excellent performance as a girl of doubtful reputation who makes good. Tough but tender, she was unsurpassable in such a part.

Apart from her bravura showing in *Sorry Wrong Number* (1948) her great days were coming to an end. True, she made several more films but the scripts became more and more trite. *Cattle Queen of Montana* (1954) with future president Ronald Reagan caused no furore and neither did *The Violent Men* (1955), even if she did allow her invalid husband, played by none other than Edward G. Robinson, to burn to death by snatching his crutches just as he was about to make his escape from a burning ranch-house. It was a re-union with Robinson with whom she had acted in *Double Indemnity* (1944), one of her great films.

She was back with Joel McCrea in *Trooper Hook* (1957) and then came her last big screen Western, *Forty Guns* (1957).

Barbara Stanwyck in Cattle Queen of Montana. *In this 1954 production she was partnered by Ronald Reagan (Benedict Bogeans/RKO).*

In 1965 she commenced a TV series, *The Big Valley*, which ran for three years. For this she won many well-deserved rewards and amused herself by acting every other actor and actress off the box.

Still active, she recently appeared in the TV adaptation of the best-selling novel, *The Thorn Birds*.

Barbara Stanwyck, hands on hips, plays The Maverick Queen *in the 1956 movie (Republic).*

High Noon on the Prairies

The Western was now half-a-century old and it might be said to have come of age. Pandering to children's Saturday matinées was on the decline, although Audie Murphy made nearly fifty 'B' movies, and kids in their millions were swarming into cinemas to see the light-hearted capers of Fess Parker as *Davy Crockett* (1955).

Much more important in the field of Westerns were films featuring Alan Ladd, William Holden, Glenn Ford and Yul Brynner.

The petticoat pistoleers were well represented in this period by Jean Arthur, Maureen O'Hara and the sex symbol Jane Russell.

He Walked Tall: Alan Ladd

Once upon a time there was an actor who had been called 'Tiny' at school. In those days he was not so embarrassed by his lack

Right: In Shane *Alan Ladd was the archetypal lone rider with two-gun justice in his holsters, moseying in from out of nowhere and finally cantering away into the far distance with never a backward glance. Made in 1953, directed by George Stevens, it is still today one of the best Westerns ever made (Paramount).*

Opposite: Carroll Baker crosses her lovely legs and glances provocatively at Alan Ladd in The Carpetbaggers *which, made in 1964, was Alan's last film. In it he played Nevada Smith, an over-the-hill Western film star. A sequel was later made under the title* Nevada Smith, *with Steve McQueen as Smith. The year was 1966 (Embassy).*

of inches as he was later to be, for in 1934 after graduating from North Hollywood High he borrowed 150 dollars and opened a hamburger stand called 'Tiny's Patio'.

The enterprise lasted about twelve months and then Tiny, who had been born in Arkansas on 3 September 1913, had to look for another job. He found one on the Warner Bros lot at a salary of 42.50 dollars a week. Hard work did not come amiss to the youngster for despite his small stature – he was five feet six inches tall – he had a muscular frame, having been a champion swimmer at school.

Proximity to the actors parading before the cameras inspired in the youth the hope that one day *he* might cavort with the best of them. To improve his chances of film fame he started to study drama.

He persevered until he obtained some local radio and stage work and a few movie bit parts. Spurring him on was the fact that he was already married with a young son, Alan Jr, but try as he may he could not catch the eye of a talent scout. Instead he caught the ear of an agent who, having heard him on radio, was much taken with his clear, precise diction. Her name was Sue Carol and from the moment she called him to her office his yearning to be a film star was to be fulfilled. His name was Alan Ladd.

Sue Carol, now on her third marriage, had been a promising young starlet. Among her many films she had played opposite George O'Brien in *The Lone Star Ranger* but she had given up acting to be an agent and now she was doing very well, always on the lookout for stray talent. When the rather poker-faced handsome young man entered her office she knew she had struck gold.

It was she who guided Alan to the heights. He was a star for six years before he first played the lead in a Western, *Whispering Smith* (1948), a special agent employed by the railroad, by which time he and his first wife had been divorced and he was married to Sue Carol.

Alan appeared in several Westerns, both before and after he became a star, but when one thinks today of Ladd and Westerns one film springs to mind, *Shane* (1953), directed by George Stevens. It is a true Western classic in every sense, the lonely gunfighter, drifting aimlessly, the pioneer family struggling to make a living

from the land, the cattle-baron determined to drive them away and the black-garbed killer he hires to do his dirty work.

It was a personal triumph for Alan Ladd who walked real tall in this one. He was never to repeat the success although he made many films after *Shane*. He started to drink heavily and became very depressed and morose. In 1962 he was found in his home bleeding heavily from a near-fatal gunshot wound. It was written down as an accident and perhaps it was.

He recovered but was never really well again. He managed to put in a very creditable appearance as a fading cowboy film star in *The Carpetbaggers* (1964) with George Peppard which was released when Alan was already dead. For the last ten days of his life he was living alone in his house in Palm Springs attended only by his butler. At half-past three in the afternoon of Wednesday 28 January 1964, his butler found him dead in bed.

He had died of an overdose of sedatives on top of a heavy drinking session.

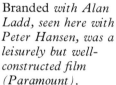

Branded *with Alan Ladd, seen here with Peter Hansen, was a leisurely but well-constructed film* (Paramount).

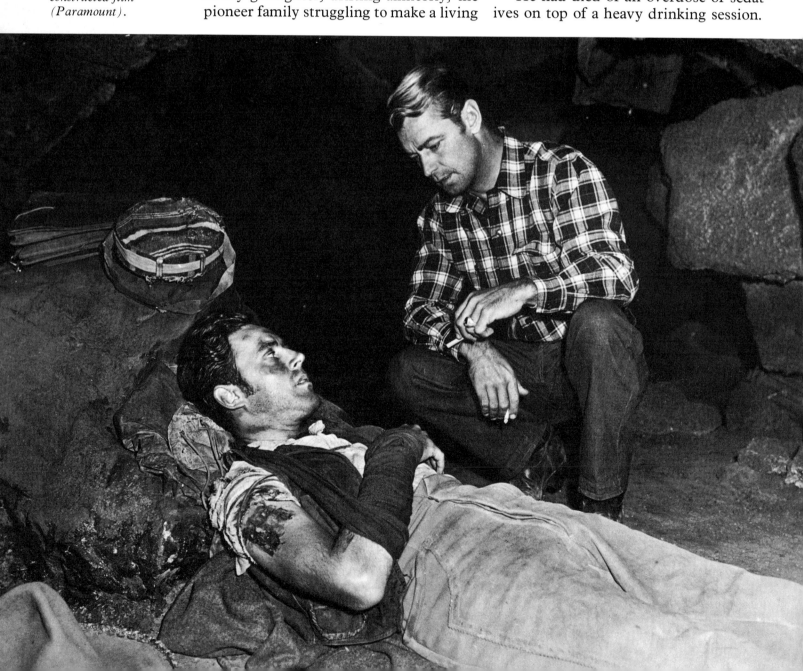

Texas Kid: Audie Murphy

At a certain Veterans' Hospital in San Antonio, Texas there stands a four-ton bronze statue of World War Two's most decorated American soldier. In a room at that hospital can be seen the many medals won by the young hero.

The hospital is the Audie L. Murphy Memorial Veterans' Hospital and it bears the name of the gallant infantryman who was decorated on 24 different occasions.

Audie Leon Murphy was born in 1924, one of nine brothers and sisters, the children of a poor sharecropper who lived near Kingston, Texas. Audie was fifteen when his father took off for pastures new, whereupon the stripling borrowed a rifle and hunted game for the family stewpot.

Came the war and Audie, after successfully persuading his doubtful sister Corinne to falsify his enlistment papers, joined the army.

He fought through Sicily and north-wards through Italy. Commissioned as a lieutenant, he later battled in the French and Austrian theatres of war. He was wounded three times, earned 24 medals which included the United States' highest military award, the Congressional Medal of Honour. He won this for clambering on to a tank destroyer and armed with a machine gun fought to a standstill 250 Germans reinforced by six tanks.

Boyishly handsome, could Hollywood possibly have resisted the national appeal of such a hero? He appeared for the first time on screen in *Beyond Glory* in 1947. *Texas, Brooklyn and Heaven* in which he was paired with Guy Madison followed in 1948, and then amazingly some not over-bright casting director conceived the notion that America's No. 1 should star as a dedicated criminal. Lloyd Nolan as the head of a boys' rehabilitation ranch recognizes something deep, deep down in the

vicious soul of the youngster and guides him to the rewarding path of virtue. In spite of this, the film managed to achieve some measure of success.

A bad kid? thought Universal-International. What could be better for his next movie in 1950 than the part of the young desperado who has immortalized the word 'Kid' in Western history? Yes, *The Kid from Texas* (also known as *Texas Kid, Outlaw*) featured Audie Murphy as Billy the Kid. This was to be the first step in the process of building Audie up into a major Western star. Accordingly, along

came *Sierra* and *Kansas Raiders* the same year. Just to ram home the fact that type-casting was something Hollywood always enjoyed, in the latter film Audie was a whitewashed Jesse James.

That sagacious director John Huston had been watching Audie's progress and borrowed him in 1951 to star in a Metro-Goldwyn-Mayer epic *The Red Badge of Courage*. Despite brutal mutilation of the finished product by the studio, the film still managed to be a success, unforgettable in every respect.

Still under contract to Universal-

International, Audie then hit the trail back to that studio and made eight Westerns. In 1955 Tony Curtis was offered the part of Audie Murphy in *To Hell and Back*, which had been the title of Audie's autobiography. Curtis refused the role and the way was open for Audie to play himself. With quiet modesty, he performed splendidly, the battle sequences were magnificently mounted and the film was a winner.

He was now established as a Hollywood star. Along the way, he had married actress Wanda Hendrix in 1949. They were divorced in 1950 and the next year he married Pamela Archer, an airline stewardess who three years previously had been responsible for Audie's movie debut by sending his photograph to James Cagney's brother, William, at the same time suggesting he should be given a screen test.

In his films, Audie Murphy could project a winning personality as epitomized in *Destry* in 1954, the remake of James Stewart's *Destry Rides Again*. When his film star days were over, he became a law enforcement officer for the Port Hueneme police department in California.

The 1950s were Audie's best years in movies. During the next decade, however, he suffered an eclipse and his films declined in quality. The one-time acknowledged King of the B-Westerns was no longer a monarch of all he surveyed.

His private life, too, was troubled. The two and a half million bucks he had made during the great days had vanished. He had always been open-handed in his financial dealings and unlucky in his investments. His marriage to Pamela broke up and he wallowed in a morass of debt.

On 28 May 1971, he boarded a chartered aircraft with five other men in Atlanta, Georgia. It crashed near Roanoke, Virginia and Audie died with the others.

Today he lies buried with America's greatest warriors in Arlington National Cemetery.

Golden Boy: William Holden

Alan Ladd was not the only star to make at least one memorable Western and to die as a result of too much alcohol. Another was William Holden. On the morning of Monday 16 November 1981, his dead body was discovered in a welter of blood in his Santa Monica apartment. It was deduced from the amount of vodka he had consumed that he must have fallen and struck his head on the corner of a bedside table. Some bloodstained tissues indicated that he had unavailingly tried to staunch the flow of blood. He had then either passed out from over-drinking or loss of blood and had died within half-an-hour.

William Holden was born William Franklin Beedle in the town of O'Fallon, Illinois, on 17 April 1918. As John Wayne's father was advised by his doctor to migrate to California for his health's sake, so was five-year-old Billy Beedle's dad which was why the family, including Billy's two brothers Dick and Bob, moved to Monrovia, twenty miles east of Los Angeles. Later they lived in South Pasadena and Bill attended South Pasadena High School and Pasadena Junior College.

It was while he was playing the eighty-year-old father of Madame Curie in a college play that he was spotted by a scout for Paramount, tested and placed under contract. His debut, a two-word bit part in *Million Dollar Legs* (1939), was not very auspicious but later that same year Columbia borrowed him to star in *Golden Boy* (1939), a film based on a Clifford Odets' play. Bill was called upon to play the part of a youngster devoted to boxing and to the violin but finding it difficult to decide which profession he should adopt.

Bill, now William Holden, earned little applause for his acting and the film was only a mediocre success. Even so Bill was offered parts in three more films and started to gain the experience he needed for stardom. Then came his first Western, *Arizona* (1940), with Glenn Ford and Claire Trevor.

Above: Two years after The Wild Bunch *in 1971, William Holden went wild again, this time as a world-weary cowboy turned amateur bank robber in* Wild Rovers. *He winds up biting the dust (Mirisch-Alpha).*

Left: In Arizona, *which went before the cameras in 1940, William Holden starred opposite Jean Arthur. It was a big film in every respect but too long for its own good (Columbia).*

Tourists in Arizona have good cause to thank Columbia for this first William Holden Western for a few miles outside Tucson the studio erected a huge set which was nothing less than a small Western town. When the film was finished, Old Tucson, as the set came to be named, remained standing. Since then many films have been shot there, among them John Wayne's *Rio Lobo* and all the exterior scenes for the popular TV series *The High Chaparral*.

Bill Holden and Glenn Ford became friends during the making of *Arizona* and remained so until Bill died. Police searching his apartment after his death found a note on which was written Ford's telephone number. The two had recently been discussing another film they would make together.

After *Arizona*, Bill made eight Westerns, including John Ford's *The Horse Soldiers* (1959) with John Wayne. Then came *The Wild Bunch* for Warner Bros (1969). This was one of Hollywood's 'big ones', starring Holden, Robert Ryan, Ernest Borgnine, Ben Johnson, Warren Oates, Strother Martin and Albert Dekker. It was directed by Sam Peckinpah and although when first released it was catechised for its explicit violence, it is today considered to be one of the most brilliant of all Westerns.

Bill Holden married the film actress Brenda Marshall in 1941, and they had three children. He died a very wealthy man with huge investments in several countries. Not for nothing was he known to all his friends by the nickname of 'Golden' Holden.

Above: At the beginning of The Wild Bunch *William Holden leads his bandits, including (and seen here) Ernest Borgnine and Warren Oates, into town on a hell-fire raid and from there on the film never loses its pace. The finale, in which the outlaws die to a man, fighting heroically against Mexican guerillas, is one of the bloodiest ever filmed. The film was made in 1969 (Warner Bros.-Seven Arts).*

Opposite: The Wild Bunch, *directed by Sam Peckinpah, was inspired by an original idea by Lee Marvin.*

Friendly but Deadly: Glenn Ford

Glenn Ford, Bill Holden's good friend, has made three times as many Westerns as Bill did. He was born in Quebec, Canada, on May Day 1916, real name Gwyllyn Samuel Newton Ford. When he was a schoolboy his family moved to Los Angeles. Bitten by the acting bug, he joined various touring companies and learned his trade the hard way. His first film was *Heaven with a Barbed Wire Fence* (1939), followed closely by *Arizona* (1940).

He followed this up very nicely with a string of 'B' movies, then enlisted in the Marine Corps when the US entered the War. His first Western when he returned to Hollywood was *The Man from Colorado* (1948). Since then he has made more than a score of Westerns, his best known being *The Fastest Gun Alive* (1956), *3.10 to Yuma* (1957), *Cowboy* (1958), *The Sheepman* (1958), the remake of Richard Dix's *Cimarron* (1960) and *Santee* (1972).

As with John Wayne, one always knows what to expect of him. His cowpokes are always casual, friendly, softly-spoken, the gentle demeanour hiding the danger that lurks within. He was particularly effective in this type of part in *Smith!* (1969) in which he played a stubborn farmer joining forces with Chief Dan George to protect the life of a young Indian accused of murder and tracked down by an Indian-hating lawman. As usual Glenn seemed to be wearing the same sombrero that he does in all his Westerns. He styles it on the type of headgear always worn by that witty

cowboy from Oklahoma, Will Rogers. Ford as a lad worked as a stablehand on Rogers' ranch and the good-natured actor solved the problem of what to do with his old hats by passing them on to the youngster when he had finished with them.

In 1943 Glenn married Eleanor Powell, famous for her twinkling feet and the three *Broadway Melody* films she made. Their son Peter co-starred with his father in the TV series *Cade's County* (1972–1974). Eleanor and Glenn were divorced in 1959, and he married Katharine Hays, from whom he was divorced in 1968.

Opposite: Smith! *was a 1969 Walt Disney Western with Glenn Ford, here with Chief Dan George (© Walt Disney Productions).*

Left: Glenn Ford huntin' an' fishin' in California's Sierra Nevada mountains.

Below: In 1960 Glenn Ford played the crusading publisher in a remake of Cimarron *(Edmund Grainger Productions/MGM).*

Bald Badman: Yul Brynner

If one film, *Shane*, stands out starkly in Alan Ladd's repertoire as his most notable, so does *The Magnificent Seven* (1960) in Yul Brynner's and this despite his resounding success in *The King and I* (1956).

Yul was born on 12 July 1915, his place of birth being generally supposed to have been Sakhalin, an island off the Siberian coast. His story starts with mystery and indeed he appears out of an unknown past in 1941 when he first appeared in the States. Stories prevail that he is the son of a Manchurian married to a gypsy girl, that he was once a wandering minstrel singing love songs, that later he became a high trapeze artiste, that he attended the Sorbonne in Paris, that he was stage manager and actor with a Parisian repertory com-

pany and that he came to the United States in 1941 where he commenced his acting career. Little of this, though, has been confirmed. Like Chris, the character he plays in *The Magnificent Seven*, he seems to have suddenly appeared, waiting for his big moment.

In real life this came to Yul when he was a television producer in New York and was given the chance of playing in a musical remake of *Anna and the King of Siam* (1946), a Rex Harrison/Irene Dunne drama. On the night that *The King and I* opened on Broadway with Yul as a strutting royal baldhead he became a top star. The Hollywood version, made in 1956, brought to him the acclaim of millions of people all over the world. Today, he is still frequently seen in stage re-presentations of the operetta.

All in all, he was an unlikely recruit for the role of master gunman in *The Magni-ficent Seven*. His reversion to the black outfit of Hopalong Cassidy was not unique, but who had ever seen a cowboy hero with a hairless pate before? If it was a visual drawback, Yul refused to recognize it. After all, he could have worn a wig as he did when playing Jean Lafitte the pirate in *The Buccaneer* (1958). That he did not and that it mattered not is a tribute to his splendid acting.

Who does not today remember the other six actors who made up The Magnificent Seven? There was Steve McQueen as cool killer Vin, Charles Bronson as Bernardo O'Reilly, half Mexican, half Irish, devoted to children, Brad Dexter as Harry who refuses to believe that Chris has taken on their dangerous assignment for any other reason but money, Robert Vaughan as Lee, the consummate gunman who has lost his nerve, James Coburn as Britt the unerring knife-thrower and

Opposite: A lone figure with hands hovering over gun-butts, Yul Brynner makes a formidable figure in The Magnificent Seven *(Mirisch-Alpha).*

Magnificent in all respects, The Magnificent Seven *had taken as its theme that of the Japanese classic* The Seven Samurai *and transposed the scene of action to the US-Mexican border. Yul Brynner gathers together the Seven which include Steve McQueen, James Coburn and Charles Bronson.*

Horst Buchholz as Chico, no great shakes as a gunman but determined to tag along with Chris.

Based on the Japanese film *The Seven Samurai* (1954), directed by Akira Kurosawa, *The Magnificent Seven*, directed by John Sturges, was one of the most successful Western movies, giving birth to three sequels, *Return of the Seven* (1966), again with Yul, *Guns of the Magnificent Seven* (1969) with George Kennedy as Chris and *The Magnificent Seven Ride!* (1972) starring Lee Van Cleef as Chris, now a married man. All four *Seven* films were packed with action depicting the triumph of determined and outnumbered men fighting against overwhelming odds. Perhaps the first was the best not only because the casting of the Seven was much better than in the three sequels but also because Calvera, the giggling homicidal bandit, was played by superb-as-ever Eli Wallach.

Yul Brynner has gone on to make more Westerns, including *Invitation to a Gunfighter* (1964), over-garrulous and slow-moving, and *Villa Rides!* (1968) which was a lively actioner, further enlivened by the presence of Robert Mitchum, and *Catlow* (1971). But *The Magnificent Seven* stands out supreme.

Above: Louis L'Amour has for years been top author in the Western field. Not for nothing, because his books invariably are of sound construction and characterization. Directed by Sam Wanamaker, Catlow, based on one of L'Amour's novels and starring Yul Brynner, was of little consequence, however. A disappointment for all L'Amour fans (Frontier Films Production).

Right: Jeff Corey in the background is not interested in the slightest in Daliah Levi's nibbling of Yul Brynner's ear in Catlow. *Perhaps Jeff suspects that the film was somewhat nonsensical.*

Wild Western Women: Jean Arthur, Maureen O'Hara and Jane Russell

As far back as the silent days Jean Arthur was appearing in Westerns. Her first was an opus delighting in the title of *Biff Bang Buddy* (1924), and for three decades she spanned the Western field, winding up with *Shane* (1953).

She was born on 17 October 1905 in New York and christened alliteratively Gladys Georgianna Greene. She was the daughter of a professional photographer which obviously was why she began modelling for photographers even while she was still at school. She appeared in an advertisement which was spotted by one of the talent scouts from Fox and given a screen-test. This earned her a contract for one year when she did little more than attract sufficient attention to be given

small parts in films for the next ten years. John Ford used her in *Cameo Kirby* (1923) which concerned the adventures of a chivalrous riverboat gambler but was unimpressed with her performance.

Ford was to change his opinion of the lively young lady twelve years later when it came to casting *The Whole Town's Talking* (1935). It was a tip-top comedy, the best of the year, with Edward G. Robinson opposite Jean. She was so good that she received the part of a quick-talking girl rooting for Gary Cooper in *Mr. Deeds Goes to Town* (1936). That same year she was paired with Gary Cooper again in *The Plainsman*. As Calamity Jane she was a wow with pistol and bullwhip. She was outstanding again

When Cecil B. DeMille planned The Plainsman *as a filmic tribute to the prowess of Wild Bill Hickok, he cast Gary Cooper as Hickok. Jean Arthur romped along as Calamity Jane wielding a nifty whip. It was filmed in 1936 (Adolf Zukor/Paramount).*

Adolph Zukor presents
GARY COOPER
JEAN ARTHUR

in Cecil B. DeMille's "THE PLAINSMAN"

with JAMES ELLISON · CHARLES BICKFORD · HELEN BURGESS · PORTER HALL
Directed by Cecil B. DeMille
A Paramount Picture

Opposite: McLintock! *filmed in 1963 was another John Wayne/ Maureen O'Hara Western. In this riotous scene Maureen dances a light fandango on the table at an open-air feast (Batjac).*

Right: Van Heflin, Jean Arthur, Brandon De Wilde and Alan Ladd in a clip from Shane *(Paramount).*

Below: Maureen O'Hara, the red-headed colleen from the Emerald Isle, was a favourite co-star of John Wayne. They are here seen together in John Ford's Rio Grande *in 1950 (Argosy/Republic Pictures).*

in *Mr. Smith Goes to Washington*, this time waiting for James Stewart.

She teamed up with William Holden and Glenn Ford in *Arizona* (1940) and with John Wayne in *A Lady Takes a Chance* (1943), a modern Western in which Wayne played a broncho-buster and she the girl from the big city who fell in love with him.

It had all been a pathway to *Shane* in which she wins the heart of the pilgrim gunman (Alan Ladd) simply by conveying with her eyes the affection his quiet loneliness has aroused in her. No words of love pass between them but one will always remember the haunted look on her face as Shane rides away for the last time.

It was only natural that John Ford, that lover of all things Irish, would be attracted to the Hibernian beauty of Maureen O'Hara. When he teamed her with John Wayne in *Rio Grande* (1950) he launched a movie partnership that was to rival that of Errol Flynn and Olivia De Havilland. Right away in *Rio Grande* the relationship is established, that of a woman with a mind of her own surrendering lovingly to the stronger will of her chosen mate.

Wayne and O'Hara were so successful together that Ford starred them in four more of his big ones, *The Quiet Man* (1952), *The Wings of Eagles* (1957), *McLintock!* (1963) and *Big Jake* (1971).

Maureen FitzSimons is a full-blooded

Irish woman, born in Dublin on 17 August 1920. She learned her profession in that most testing of all acting academies, Dublin's Abbey School. She was only nineteen when she left the school to act with Charles Laughton in *Jamaica Inn* (1939), directed by Alfred Hitchcock. Charles had a high opinion of her acting ability and took her with him to Hollywood to play Esmeralda in *The Hunchback of Notre Dame* (1940).

She cowered before Laughton's indescribably ugly and misshapen menace to such good effect that she was never kept waiting long for film roles for the next thirty-two years.

Her participation in her nine Westerns has always been more than commendable, sincere and deeply loving in *Buffalo Bill* with Joel McCrea and boisterous in *Big Jake* with Wayne.

Her brother Charles FitzSimons was the producer of *The Deadly Companions* (1961). It was directed by Sam Peckinpah and was not one of her happiest experiences. The fiery Sam quarrelled with FitzSimons to such an extent that the producer forbade the director even to speak to his sister. The story line called for Maureen's co-star Brian Keith as Yellow-

leg, a veteran of the Civil War, to shoot accidentally the son of a saloon girl. Most of the film concerns itself with Yellowleg trying to make amends by transporting the boy's body for miles across a desert, through Indian country, so that the son can be buried with his father. The role of a saloon girl was a grim part for Maureen, but she proved more than equal to it even under the difficulty of working for a director who had been instructed not to parley with her.

Her last Western was *Big Jake* with Wayne. Since then Maureen has not been active on the screen.

She has been married three times, first to George Brown, then to Will Price by whom she had a daughter, Bronwyn, then to Charles Blair.

Virginia O'Brien was famous for her deadpan expression, Martha Raye for her prodigious mouth, Betty Grable for her legs. It was left to Jane Russell to render notorious her immense bosom. When her first film, *The Outlaw* (1943), was at last exhibited after being banned for three years by the over-zealous Hays office, the boys were goggle-eyed and the girls mighty envious.

Jane was to exploit her visible talents

When a bunch of kidnappers hold Big Jake's grandson to ransom, they're bound to be run down to a bloody shoot-out. What else could they have expected, for Big Jake was played by John Wayne. Maureen O'Hara was his wife and Richard Boone the ruthless outlaw chief (Big Jake, Batjac/Cinema Center Films 1971).

to good measure in the years that followed that mediocre film, which had been yet another glamorizing of the little thug who went by the name of Billy the Kid.

She came into the world on 21 June 1921, her given names being Ernestine Jane Geraldine. She hails from Bemidji, Minnesota and after leaving school, began work as a chiropodist's assistant then took up modelling and studied acting at Max Reinhardt's Theatrical Workshop and with Maria Ouspenskaya, the Russian founder of the School of Dramatic Arts.

From scores of applicants for the role of the girl who climbs into bed with delirious Billy the Kid to keep him warm,

Jane was personally chosen by Howard Hughes, that strange multi-multi-millionaire aviator turned film-producer. She soared to instant stardom and has made more than a score of films.

Developing into a first-rate light comedy actress, she played opposite Bob Hope in *The Paleface* (1948) and with Bob again and Roy Rogers in *Son of Paleface* (1952). In *Montana Belle* (1952), as Belle Starr the infamous woman outlaw, she was repeating her previous performance as a bandit in *Son of Paleface*, this time as the crony of the Daltons.

Jane married Bob Waterfield in 1943 and they have three children.

Much bally-hoo concerning the mammary charms of Jane Russell accompanied the release of The Outlaw *in 1943, yet another Billy the Kid saga, no nearer the truth than any of the others preceding it (Howard Hughes).*

The Sun Sets on the West

In the new-style Westerns of the 1960s and '70s, fair play was out. If villains chose to fight dirty, then so did the men opposing them. If a man had a price on his head, no questions were asked; the sooner he was dead, the sooner the reward could be collected.

Since the 1960s this has been the truer to life, down-to-earth philosophy of many Western films. Not always commendable, but a much closer approximation to the old West than the stereotyped sagebrushers of pre-war days which were designedly romantic and more naive.

Not that, as we approach the mid-1980s, there are all that many Westerns to discuss, in these terms or any other. It seems as if Westerns may even be heading for the last round-up. Replacing them are films devoted to cops and robbers, spies, astronauts and disco ravers. Since 1971 an average of no more than twelve Westerns a year have been made, and in 1982 there were only two.

Declining cinema audiences, the huge costs involved in making movies, and competition from television have hit the Western as hard as other types of film. Perhaps harder, for the Western today is history.

Acrobatic Actor: Burt Lancaster

Burt Lancaster, ex-circus acrobat and floorwalker, was 'discovered' riding up in an elevator in New York, on his way to meet Norma Anderson, the girl who was to become his wife and whom he had met when she was entertaining the US forces in Italy during the war. A fellow passenger in the elevator was Jack Mahlor, a theatrical producer, who was impressed by his athletic figure and toughly handsome features.

Mahlor asked Burt if he would care to audition for the part of a swaggering sergeant in a war play entitled *The Sound of Hunting*. Burt was given the role and although the drama ran for only thirteen performances, he received during that time no less than seven Hollywood film offers.

His first film, *Desert Fury* (1947), was an indifferent production starring Mary Astor as a gambling boss and Lizabeth Scott as her headstrong daughter. Burt hovered around as a young sheriff in love with the daughter. The producers, Paramount, held the film back for a year which is why *The Killers* (1946), Mark Hellinger's morose adaptation of Ernest Hemingway's crime story, is considered to be Burt's movie debut. It was an instant hit with public and critics and Burt was launched into star rating.

He had been born on 2 November 1913 in East Harlem, New York, the youngest of five children born to a Post Office official. He was to have five children himself in due course. Early on, Burton Stephen Lancaster attended the De Witt Clinton High School and from there won a scholarship to New York University. After two years, he walked out with a diminutive school pal named Nick Cravat to join the modest Kay Brothers Circus in Petersburg, Virginia. They partnered each other in an acrobatic act and made a precarious living, during which time Burt married – briefly – a young acrobat, June Ernst. Seven years later in St Louis he

Opposite: Jane Russell admires and enjoys the warbling of Roy Rogers while tenderfoot Bob Hope looks on jealously. This is a scene from Son of Paleface *which, made in 1952, was a sequel to the equally popular* The Paleface *which had been filmed four years previously and also starred Jane and Bob (Paramount).*

injured his right hand and took a job as a floorwalker in the ladies' underwear department in Marshall Field's store in Chicago.

In 1942 Burt joined the Army and, because of his circus experience, was posted to the Special Services Division of the Fifth Army to entertain the troops in North Africa, Italy and Austria.

Once into the movies business, he was one of the first film stars to form his own production company, Norma Productions Inc., in 1948.

Burt's first Western was *Vengeance Valley* (1951) with Robert Walker and Joanne Dru who had already won her spurs in three memorable Westerns, *Red River* and *She Wore a Yellow Ribbon* both with John Wayne, and John Ford's *Wagonmaster* (1950). Walker was at his best as Burt's brother, a simpering rogue and the type of role in which he excelled. He died the same year, aged only 37, a victim of alcoholism.

Lancaster went on to make many fine Westerns, from *Apache* (1954) as an irreconcilable Indian, through *Vera Cruz* (1954) riling Gary Cooper for all he was worth, to *The Kentuckian* (1955) as a romping pioneer in fringed buckskin and so to the sombre *Gunfight at the O.K.*

Above: The story of Vengeance Valley *calls for John Ireland to believe that Burt Lancaster is responsible for his sister's pregnancy. The quarrel results in this savage fight (MGM).*

Left: Henry Brandon doesn't think much of Burt Lancaster's drinking habits in this incident from Vera Cruz, *1954. Hanging around in this movie was Charles Buchinsky. When* Vera Cruz *was in the can he changed his name to Bronson (Hecht-Lancaster).*

Opposite: From The Killers *in 1946, Burt Lancaster has turned in one sparkling performance after another (Hal B. Wallis Productions).*

Above: In The Professionals *Burt Lancaster and Lee Marvin are determined to pluck from the grasp of bandit Jack Palance the sultry charms of Claudia Cardinale and return her to her husband. Easier said than done, though (Pax).*

Right: Cattle Annie and Little Britches *was produced in 1980, starring Amanda Plummer and Diane Lane as Annie and Little Britches respectively with Burt Lancaster, here seen cuddling the little nuisances, and Rod Steiger (King Hitzig Productions/Hendale/United Artists Theaters).*

Corral (1957). In this last film he was brilliant in the type of role that filmgoers have come to admire most, the friendly amiable man with glinting eyes and flashing teeth and a scarcely controlled inner drive and willingness for violence. When he unleashes his fury in the O.K. Corral he is at his frightening best.

He was so good in his tempestuous role as a hypocritical revivalist striving to contain his lechery in *Elmer Gantry* (1960) that he won the Academy Award for best actor.

He was at it again in *The Professionals* (1966) when he set out with Lee Marvin, Robert Ryan and Woody Strode to rescue the curvaceous Claudia Cardinale from the greedy clutches of Jack Palance. This film, with its accent on violence and on sex, as registered by a Mexican woman delightedly baring her breasts under a makeshift open-air shower, is typical of the 'adult' Western we know so well today.

Burt Lancaster is still making films. He may not be as sprightly as once he was, his role changing to that of an ageing leader of a gang in *Cattle Annie and Little Britches* (1979),but his wicked grin is still as formidable as ever.

The Nameless Men:
Clint Eastwood and Lee Van Cleef

In San Francisco on 31 May 1930 the happy marriage of Ruth and Clinton Eastwood was blessed by the arrival of a baby boy. Clint, a company executive, gave his son his own name and reckoned that there was a fair chance the youngster would follow in his footsteps and be a business administrator.

At school, boy Clint was a dedicated athlete, his particular sport being basketball. He was also interested in jazz, fast cars and motorcycles, but certainly not in the art dramatic.

After graduation, anxious to flex his muscles, he took off for Oregon and worked there as a lumberjack. Then, in

In quick succession in 1964, 1965 and 1966 Serge Leone was responsible for three box-office block-busters, A Fistful of Dollars, For a Few Dollars More *and* The Good, the Bad and the Ugly. *All were graced by the inscrutable presence of Clint Eastwood. The second and third films recruited Lee Van Cleef and he and Clint made a duo that will be long remembered. Here they are exchanging confidences in* The Good, the Bad and the Ugly *(PEA).*

common with thousands of other young Americans, he received one day a communication beginning 'Greetings', ostensibly from that distinguished guardian of the country's well-being, the President. In other words, he was drafted.

Clint once hitch-hiked a flight in a naval plane from Seattle to Port Ord, where he was stationed. Engine trouble developed and the plane ditched in the sea off Point Keyes, California. The pilot had a Mae West life-jacket, Clint did not. He must have thanked his lucky stars that he was a powerful swimmer, for he had to swim three miles to shore.

While in the army, he became firm friends with another draftee, David Meyer. David was interested in film work and had already been in contact with Universal Studios. He was to become better known as David Janssen, the star of many movies and the popular TV series *The Fugitive*.

When Clint left the army, at a loss what to do next, David suggested he should give acting a whirl and offered to introduce him to somebody at Universal. Nothing came of that initial introduction and Clint signed on at Los Angeles City College to study business methods. It was at this time, 1953, that he met and married an attractive blonde named Maggie Johnson.

Clint kept in touch with Universal, his persistence finally being rewarded with a test. A forty-week contract at a weekly salary of 75 dollars followed and he appeared in small parts in half-a-dozen films. Clint felt confident enough to ask for a raise; the studio dropped him. For the next twelve months he worked at anything, even digging swimming pools, but still beavered away at the film and television world.

Sheer luck brought him to the notice of a producer who was searching for someone to play an army cadet in what proved to be a short-lived TV series, *West Point*. His more-than-adequate performance won him the second lead in another TV series, *Rawhide*. Eric Fleming had the lead part of Gil Favor and Clint was given the role of Rowdy Yates. As Rowdy, he was soon known not only in his own country but in the world at large, even Japan.

During a break in the series in 1964 he was approached by an Italian movie-

maker, Sergio Leone, who wanted him for an Italian-financed Western to be made in Spain. The film was the celebrated *A Fistful of Dollars* (1964).

It catered primarily for the tastes of Italian and Spanish moviegoers, with bloodshed and violence galore and a minimum of dialogue, due probably to the fact that few of the actors spoke the same language. It was an international success and sent shock waves through Hollywood's studios. Because of its Italian derivation, it was labelled a 'spaghetti' Western, a term that has survived to this day.

In Leone's films, Clint plays the part of The Man with No Name, unshaven, a serape draped over his shoulders, a flat-crowned hat shading his slitted eyes and a

Above: Marianne Koch provided the feminine interest in A Fistful of Dollars *(Jolly-Constantin-Ocean).*

Opposite: Clint Eastwood as he appeared in the 'spaghetti' Western For a Few Dollars More, *made in 1965 (PEA Productions/Constantin/ Arturo Gonzales).*

Below: Clint Eastwood's macho Westerns ran out of Steam with High Plains Drifter *in 1972 (Universal/Malpaso Company).*

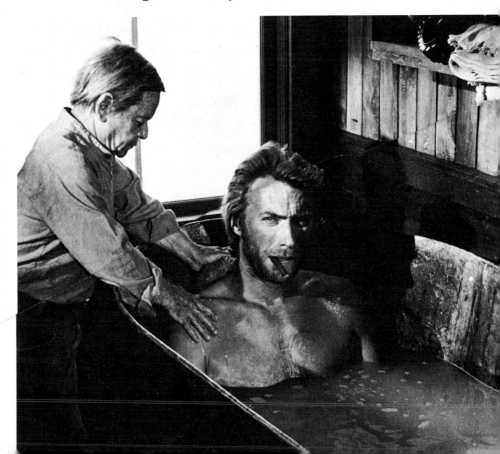

half-smoked cigarillo drooping from the corner of his mouth. From out of nowhere he would ride into town on a mule and it would not be long before he would be out-drawing the local gun-talent and treating all and sundry to a most incredible display of marksmanship.

A Fistful of Dollars gave birth to a sequel, *For a Few Dollars More*. For this blood-bath, Leone brought in a balding, sneering man with Oriental eyes to match Clint's gun-magic. His name was Lee Van Cleef and he had been playing in Holly-wood Westerns off and on for thirteen years, ever since his first appearance in Gary Cooper's *High Noon*.

For a Few Dollars More was succeeded by *The Good, the Bad and the Ugly* when Eli Wallach joined the redoubtable East-wood and Lee van Cleef. All three 'Man with No Name' movies were big money-makers. That was more than enough for

United Artists back in Hollywood to mount their own spaghetti-type Western for Clint Eastwood. *Hang 'Em High* it was called and when it was released in 1968 it regained its entire cost within ten weeks. It was a record for United Artists.

Clint felt confident enough after this to found his own production company. In-stantly he broke away from the brutal blood-drenched Westerns, so beloved by the Italians. Instead he produced, under the direction of Don Siegel, *Coogan's Bluff* (1968) in which Clint was a modern-day Western sheriff posted to New York to bring back a wanted criminal.

Then came a complete break from Westerns. With Richard Burton, he starred in the gigantic *Where Eagles Dare* (1969), a World War Two adventure film based on Alistair MacLean's best-selling thriller.

From then on, Clint Eastwood could be

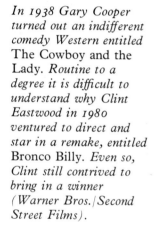

In 1938 Gary Cooper turned out an indifferent comedy Western entitled The Cowboy and the Lady. *Routine to a degree it is difficult to understand why Clint Eastwood in 1980 ventured to direct and star in a remake, entitled* Bronco Billy. *Even so, Clint still contrived to bring in a winner (Warner Bros./Second Street Films).*

numbered amongst the select band of super-stars. *Paint Your Wagon* confirmed his versatility. It was produced in the same year as *Where Eagles Dare*. A huge sprawling musical with Lee Marvin and Jean Seberg, Clint was called upon to sing 'I Talk to the Trees' and did so creditably.

Clint's next Western was *Two Mules for Sister Clara* which he made, again with Don Siegel, in 1970. Shirley MacLaine partnered him in this but it was not one of Clint's best.

Since then, Clint has specialized in Westerns and tough thrillers, moving blithely from one to another, all compelling, even 1980's *Bronco Billy*, another near-miss. Of particular mention are the cops-and-robbers movies, *Dirty Harry* (1971) and its sequel *Magnum Force* (1973), not forgetting two Westerns with Leone overtones, *High Plains Drifter* (1972) and *The Outlaw Josey Wales* (1976).

Lee was born in New Jersey on 9 January 1925 and went to high school but left to join the US Navy. On his discharge he worked as a labourer on the estate of millionairess Doris Duke. After that he took a job in a factory and in his spare time studied public accounting. In 1947 a friend persuaded him to participate in amateur dramatics and he took to acting like a duck takes to water. Three years later he was touring with *Mister Roberts*, the play made famous by Henry Fonda.

It was while the show was playing in Los Angeles that Stanley Kramer, the producer-director who was working on *High Noon*, noticed Lee and signed him at once for the part of one of the gunmen out to put a rapid term to the life of Will Kane, the sheriff.

His menacing stare and mirthless grin rendered him tailor-made for villainous roles and there followed several films, ranging from John Wayne's *The Conqueror*, in which he played a sinister Mongol, to *Gunfight at the O.K. Corral*

Lee Van Cleef was in his element in The Nebraskan, *which starred Phil Carey, in 1953. Lee is a deserter from the cavalry and just for good measure a cold-blooded killer. The* Nebraskan *was filmed in 3D, all the rage at the time (Columbia).*
and Jay Silverheels

with Kirk Douglas as Doc Holliday and Van Cleef as his quarry.

Later Lee was badly injured in a car crash, his left kneecap was removed, and it took him six months to walk properly again. Returning to work, he was down to his last dollar and unable to pay his telephone bill when his agent secured an interview for him with Sergio Leone.

Leone took one glance at that savage snarl and gave Lee the opportunity of rivalling Clint Eastwood in skullduggery in *For a Few Dollars More*. They later repeated their successful partnership in *The Good, the Bad and the Ugly* with Eli Wallach.

Today Lee is a wealthy man, no longer worrying about his telephone bill.

Above: In Barquero *made in 1970, Lee Van Cleef plays a goodie for a change (Aubrey Schenck).*

Opposite: The slit-eyed glower of Lee Van Cleef in The Good, the Bad and the Ugly *(PEA).*

Stoneface: Charles Bronson

When Alan Ladd one day strolled on to the set of his new Western *Drum Beat* (1954), he noticed the director Delmar Daves chatting with a six-foot-tall man with an impassive, chilly face and black shaggy hair. His narrowed eyes were forbidding and glinting. His name was Charles Buchinsky but he had recently changed it to Bronson. In *Drum Beat* he was to play a Modoc Indian chief, Captain Jack, and Daves planned to make much of that glowering battered face, for if ever a man's face was his fortune, Bronson's was.

He was born on 3 November 1921, the son of a Lithuanian immigrant and refugee from the Russian Army who was hacking out a nightmare existence as a miner in Ehrenfeld, Pennsylvania and struggling to support a wife and a bevy of children (eventually there were fifteen).

In Ehrenfeld in those days, miners' sons were expected to follow their fathers below ground and by his early teens, Charles was tunnelling away on night-shifts for a dollar a ton. As he sweated and laboured, building the muscular frame that is admired so much today, he swore that the time would come when he would better himself.

The war brought surcease, for he was drafted in 1943 and for the first time in his life could wear clean decent clothes and eat regularly. Not content with his first posting as a mess supply truck-driver in Kingman, Arizona, he volunteered for more hazardous duties and became an air gunner, flying on twenty-five missions and suffering a bullet wound in the shoulder.

The war over, he went back to Ehrenfeld but not to the mine. Instead, he toiled in a tyre factory and then as a brick-layer. He was above ground, but the jobs were just as dreary as mining.

One day he stowed away on a freight train and left Ehrenfeld, never to return. He found his way to Atlantic City and began an itinerant life, hitch-hiking across the country, working at anything that would put the odd dollar in his pocket. He eventually drifted to Philadelphia where he fell in with a few actors, members of the Play and Players Troupe, who apparently poured into his receptive ears the benefits and rewards that can be obtained from treading the boards. After Charles married Harriet Tendler, an amateur actress with the Play and Players Troupe, he and his new wife headed for Pasadena, California.

Charles managed to find a billet with the Pasadena Community Playhouse, that treasure house of actors from which the film studios had recruited so many actors.

Left: When Alan Ladd produced Drum Beat *in 1954, he gave Charles Bronson his big chance. Bronson seized it and gained the critics' praise. From then on he was marked for stardom (Jaguar Productions).*

Opposite: In Chato's Land *Charles Bronson, playing an Indian hunted by a posse, was strong but silent. This 1972 movie was directed and produced by British director Michael Winner (*Scimitar*).*

He had not been long with the Playhouse before a telephone call came from a studio asking for a character actor who looked rather like John Garfield with a touch of the Humphrey Bogart.

The film studio got Charles, and his first part of any substance was with Gary Cooper in *You're in the Navy Now* (1951);

Charles Buchinsky was in the movie world now.

He was in and out of films for the next three years until his acting as a Modoc chief in *Drum Beat* caught the attention of director Delmar Daves. Throughout the film Daves brought Charles (now Bronson) into close-up so that the camera

could linger lovingly over those battered features that looked as though they had been hewn from stone.

From then on the road led upwards for Charles. Six years later, after twelve films, including *Vera Cruz* (1954), *Jabal* (1956), *Run of the Arrow* (1957) and *Showdown at Boot Hill* (1958), he received 50,000 dollars for his not too onerous part in *The Magnificent Seven*. Several Westerns followed, *Four for Texas* (1963), *Villa Rides!* (1968), *Once Upon a Time in the West* (1969), *Chato's Land* (1972), *Breakheart Pass* (1975). Charles was never less than superb in all of them.

It was during the filming of the war epic *The Great Escape* (1963) in Bavaria that Charles met English actor David McCallum and his comely wife Jill née Ireland. Two years later Charles was divorced from his first wife, in 1966 Jill Ireland and her husband were also divorced, and in 1968 Charles and Jill were married. The next year they acted together in *Rider in the Rain* (1969) and since then have repeated the act in several films, two Westerns, *Valdez the Half-Breed* (1973) and *Breakheart Pass* being prominent amongst them.

The Noble Gunman: Gregory Peck

If today Gregory Peck is regarded as one of the screen's great heroes, his first appearance in a Western contributed nothing to that opinion.

When David O. Selznick was discussing his production *Duel in the Sun* (1946) with King Vidor the director, the latter ventured to protest at the foulness of the character Lewt whom Gregory Peck was to play. Peck had been acting in films for only two years but was already a star of magnitude, specializing in sympathetic roles of integrity. In *The Keys of the Kingdom* (1944), he had been a priest of incredible nobility, fervently spreading the Gospel, a model of rectitude. In *The Yearling* (1946), he was the gentle understanding father of a boy who had lost his heart to a young deer.

Now Selznick was insisting that this paragon of virtue should play the part of a depraved villain and Vidor wanted to inject into Lewt a last-minute contrition for all the evil he has wrought. After all, he is to die in the arms of Jennifer Jones, also mortally wounded (they have shot each other). But Selznick wouldn't listen.

To Gregory Peck's credit, he was superb in the film, at his best when, having single-handedly caused a horrifying train wreck, he rides away nonchalantly whistling 'I've been working on the railroad'. His cold-blooded action has

been triggered by the fact that the coming of the railroad is damaging the interests of Lewt's father, owner of a million-acre ranch.

Peck's portrayal of the foul Lewt contributed significantly to the success of the film, one of the most profitable Westerns ever made, as did Jennifer Jones' presentation of a sultry half-breed girl.

Peck was born on 5 April 1916 and christened Eldred Gregory Peck. His birth place was La Jolla, California, so already he was well placed for a film career. He was on stage in the early 1940s and was lured to the film world by the chance of starring in *Days of Glory* (1944). It was a sincere but somewhat turgid war film with Gregory somewhere in there between the Russians and the Nazis.

It was not a very good film but it served as Gregory Peck's springboard to instant stardom. That same year, Twentieth Century-Fox were swift to sign him up for *The Keys of the Kingdom* and the sincerity he brought to his acting ensured his elevation to that of superstar.

In his next Western, *Yellow Sky* (1948), he and Richard Widmark are leaders of a bunch of bank robbers holed up in a ghost town. A local resident is that worthy beauty Anne Baxter and although Gregory is fundamentally a baddie, he manages to save Anne from the leering

Opposite: Everything was big about The Big Country, *a truly superb Western from 1957. Carroll Baker is the cause of mutual hatred between Gregory Peck and Charlton Heston, which results in one of the most spectacular fist-fights ever (Anthony-World Wide Productions).*

Right: Gregory Peck's portrayal of a sombre doom-laden gunman in The Gunfighter, *1950, was unsurpassable. He is seen here with Millard Mitchell (Twentieth Century-Fox).*

Below: MacKenna's Gold, *an over-pretentious Western filmed in 1969, was not one of Gregory Peck's best films by a long way. Apart from Peck, Omar Sharif, Telly Savalas, Raymond Massey, Lee J. Cobb, Edward G. Robinson and Keenan Wynn were also there to share any honours the movie might have earned (Highroad Productions/Carl Foreman).*

advances and lecherous intentions of Widmark.

Again he played a character no better than he should have been in *The Gunfighter* (1950), truly a classic Western which established the figure of the now traditional gun-weary killer who has run out of time. Grim, unsmiling, the gunfighter has come to town to seek out his estranged wife and son. He has just killed a young lout anxious to earn the unenviable reputation of being the man who has killed the infamous Jimmy Ringo. Ringo's wife promises to return to him if he can last a year without gunplay. Agreeing to this compact when it can only be a matter of time before he is brought to bay once more, Ringo resignedly allows himself to be mortally wounded by the next punk who crosses his path.

Jimmy Ringo is one of the most powerful interpretations of a Western gunman ever screened. Several other Western films such as *The Big Country* (1958), *How the West Was Won* (1963), *MacKenna's Gold* (1968) and *Shoot Out* (1971), have been graced by the presence and smiling gentility of Gregory Peck but none has been so moving as *The Gunfighter*.

Gregory Peck has three children by his first wife, Greta Rice, whom he married in 1942. They were divorced in 1954 and he married Veronique Passani, who came to interview him for a magazine article, the following year. They have two children.

No-good Charmer: Paul Newman

Opposite: In the 1967 actioner Hombre, *Paul Newman was superb in the role of a taciturn paleface who has been raised by Apaches. Wooden-faced, he ignores the sneers of his co-travellers aboard a coach heading for an ambush planned by Richard Boone as leader of an outlaw gang (Hombre Productions).*

Below: Paul Newman tried his hand at Billy the Kid in The Left-Handed Gun. *Lita Milan is here seen with Paul.*

Western badmen seem to have hypnotized Hollywood producers much as snakes hypnotize rabbits. Jesse and Frank James, the Dalton Brothers, the Younger Brothers, Butch Cassidy and his Wild Bunch, Sam Bass and others have all figured again and again in movies, usually presented in a sympathetic light.

One of the most infamous, Billy the Kid, has probably been featured more than any badman, possibly because he is supposed to have sent to the Happy Hunting Grounds twenty-one men, 'not counting Mexicans and Indians', by the time he was knocked off by Sheriff Pat Garrett at the ripe old age of twenty-one.

Among actors who have taken the part of Billy are: Johnny Mack Brown, Buster Crabbe, Robert Taylor, Bob Steele, Audie Murphy, Jack Beutel, Scott Brady, Geoffrey Deuel, Kris Kristofferson and Paul Newman. Of them all, Newman's Billy has probably received the most plaudits. At least in *The Left-Handed Gun* (1958) directed by Arthur Penn, he played Billy as the neurotic sadistic killer that he probably was, even though Billy was *not* left-handed, a mistake that has been perpetuated because a well-known photograph of the Kid has always been printed in reverse.

He was born on 26 January 1925 on Shaker Heights, Ohio and was therefore at the right age to be drafted during the war. With his war service behind him, Paul studied drama at Kenyon College and

after a spell in a stock company signed on at the Yale School of Drama.

His good looks, twinkling blue eyes and natural charm soon won him work in TV studios and on the stage. He studied at the Actors' Studio and absorbed much of the Method technique but later seldom projected it as determinedly as Rod Steiger or Marlon Brando.

He was playing in *Picnic* on the Broadway stage when he was approached by Warner Bros to make *The Silver Chalice* (1955), an historical epic based on a novel by Frank G. Slaughter, and a film that Newman would rather forget.

Since then Paul has appeared in one money-maker after another, including *Cat on a Hot Tin Roof* (1958), *Exodus* (1958), *From the Terrace* (1958), *The Hustler* (1961), *Cool Hand Luke* (1967) and *The Sting* (1973).

Thanks to his unfailingly brilliant

acting, his Westerns have all been watchable even if not always complimentary to him in story lines and purpose. *Hud* (1963), directed by Martin Ritt, was a modern Western and Paul played a cocky no-good, the type of role when he can be his insolent, shiftiest best.

The Outrage (1964) was a Western remake of the Japanese classic *Rashomon*. Paul Newman played a Mexican bandit who is supposed to have raped a girl while her husband stands by, an interested onlooker. In *Hombre* (1967) Paul was a white man raised as an Indian. It was far superior to both his previous Westerns.

Two years later Robert Redford joined Paul Newman for the all-time winner *Butch Cassidy and the Sundance Kid* (1969), directed by George Roy Hill. This film, in which the two superstars appeared as a pair of rollicking bandits doomed to an untimely end, was the most phenomen-

ally successful Western ever made. Together with two of Paul's other films, *The Sting* and *The Towering Inferno* (1974), it is one of the fifteen most popular films of the century.

With real-life Westerners Billy the Kid and Butch Cassidy behind him, Paul went on to tackle two more. The first was that quaint fellow Judge Roy Bean, in *The Life and Times of Judge Roy Bean* (1972), followed by *Buffalo Bill and the Indians* (1976). With a title like that, one could have been excused for expecting a real rip-roaring Western packed with action, especially with Paul as Buffalo Bill. It was not to be. The movie was dull, over-stressing the notion that Bill Cody was an out-and-out fraud. Most certainly the old frontiersman wasn't everything the pulp magazines cracked him up to be but he wasn't that much of a shyster. Still, Paul did his best – as always.

Paul Newman was a credible Buffalo Bill in Buffalo Bill and the Indians *While Geraldine Chaplin took up the role of Annie Oakley, played previously by Barbara Stanwyck and Betty Hutton. The film was produced in 1976 (Dino de Laurentiis Corp./Lion's Gate Films/Talent Assocs.-Norton Simon).*

Man of Method: Marlon Brando

If the Hollywood moguls have taken a very lenient view of the homicidal activities of Billy the Kid and other bandits, they really excelled themselves when it came to the blood-thirsty bandit, Emiliano Zapata. Licentious, treacherous and cruel, he specialized in crucifying his victims and devising novel methods of torture almost too sickening to describe.

When it came to a film about this monster, *Viva Zapata!* (1952), the part was taken by an actor who, with only two films behind him, was already world-famous: Marlon Brando. Then, lo and behold! Emiliano Zapata became the Robin Hood of Mexico and filmgoers left

the cinemas well-nigh weeping over the unjust fate that had befallen him, a martyr to treachery on the part of his fellow-murderers.

Marlon was born in Omaha, Nebraska on 3 April 1924, the only son of Marlon and Dorothy Brando. Way back, the family had been French, the name then being spelt Brandeau. Marlon had two sisters, Frances and Jocelyn. The latter was to reach Hollywood before her more celebrated brother and at one time acted in a Western with Randolph Scott.

Irresponsible at school, difficult at home as the lad was, his father decided that young Marlon at the age of seventeen

Opposite: In One-Eyed Jacks *Marlon Brando is a young outlaw gunman betrayed by his co-bandit Karl Malden. Marlon directed this one himself, but this otherwise excellent actioner is over-long (Pennebaker 1959–61).*

should be enrolled at the Shattuck Military Academy, Faribault, Minnesota, a disastrous decision. Far from knuckling under the rigid discipline of the Academy, the headstrong cadet engaged in various pranks that finally enraged the preceptors to such an extent that he was expelled.

From the Military Academy, Marlon went to New York where he stayed with his sisters. Here he took on one or two menial jobs before deciding to follow Jocelyn's example and try his hand at acting.

She was at that time a student in the Dramatic Workshop of the New School for Social Research and Marlon joined her. At once he impressed his drama coach, Stella Adler, with the power of his brooding personality and histrionic ability which so admirably accorded with Stella's notions of what good acting was all about, notions which culminated in 'The Method'. Even today Marlon seems to be

The Method personified.

I Remember Mama was the play in which Marlon made his Broadway debut. It was a hit and Marlon remained with it for a year. He was feeling somewhat discontented with life, after performing (and quarrelling) in *The Eagle has Two Heads* with the mercurial Tallulah Bankhead who dispensed with his services in favour of Helmut Dantine, when along came Elia Kazan, the director, to persuade him to enrol with the Actors' Studio, where such combustible performers as Rod Steiger, Eli Wallach, Montgomery Clift, Marilyn Monroe, James Dean and Paul Newman all studied.

Kazan, the Good Samaritan, later introduced Marlon to Tennessee Williams who was looking for a glowering animal of an actor to portray Stanley Kowalski in his new play *A Streetcar Named Desire*. Brando's shambling, shabby, mumbling brute was something

The pretty girl enjoying a merry moment with Randolph Scott in the 1955 Western Ten Wanted Men *is none other than Jocelyn Brando, Marlon's sister (Columbia/Scott Brown Production).*

Opposite: Marlon Brando was outstanding in Viva Zapata! *a 1952 tribute to the brilliant Mexican guerilla, Emiliano Zapata, but it was Anthony Quinn as Zapata's brother Eufemio who marched off with the acting honours. He won an Oscar for best supporting actor (Twentieth Century-Fox).*

completely new to the theatre. It took Broadway by storm and a star was born.

Three years later Marlon was lured to Hollywood by the bait of a harrowing part as a war-crippled paraplegic in *The Men* (1950). The critics were lavish in their praise and they even topped their adulation the following year when he filmed *A Streetcar Named Desire.*

Marlon Brando could now pick and choose the roles he played.

He directed as well as acted in *One-Eyed Jacks* (1959–61), a masochistic film with Karl Malden gleefully smashing the outlaw-hero's gunhand. Financially the film was a failure, but over the years it has assumed something of a cult status, being unlike any Western made before it.

His next venture into the West was *The Appaloosa* (1965), released in Britain

Above: With his penchant for the bizarre, Marlon Brando made a bewildering character of a self-constituted lawman in the film Missouri Breaks, *directed by Arthur Penn (EK 1976)*

Opposite: Burt Lancaster and Lee Marvin are two of The Professionals. *A film packed with pulsating action (Pax).*

under the title *Southwest to Sonora*. It was a revenge Western, an ex-buffalo hunter turned rancher tracking down the bandit who had stolen his beloved appaloosa stallion. Short on story values, heavy with violence, it was another of Marlon's misses. It was personally disappointing to him because he made it in an attempt to highlight the way in which certain Indian tribes' rights by treaty were being flouted by the US government.

It was for the same cause that Marlon accepted the role of Robert Lee Clayton, a

bounty-hunter, in *The Missouri Breaks* (1976) with Jack Nicholson. The film did not bring in the financial rewards that Marlon had hoped he could pass along to the Indians.

Brando has won two Oscars for best actor, the first for *On the Waterfront* (1954) and the second for *The Godfather* (1972), when he first declared his stand on behalf of the American Indians by sending a young Indian woman to the Academy Awards ceremony to refuse acceptance of it.

Born to Trouble: Lee Marvin

The second son of a Great War veteran, Lee Marvin was born on 19 February 1924 in New York. From the moment the toddler discovered that feet were for moving around on fast and fists were for fighting, the pattern of his life began to formulate. He rebelled against any form of authority, and there followed expulsion from one school after another and eventually from a monastery.

Lee was seventeen when war broke out and itching for real action, so he joined the toughest unit of them all, the Marines.

Monastery or marines, it was all the same to Private Marvin, known to his brothers-in-arms as Captain Marvel or Horse-face or Dog-face. In 1944, on Saipan in the Marianas, a shell took him in the base of his spine and that was the end of Private Marvin's war and military service. He was lucky to escape life-long paralysis.

Back home with a Purple Heart medal and his discharge papers in his pocket, Lee looked round for a job. In Woodstock, outside New York, where his family were living, he took on various itinerant occupations, shovelling snow, gardening, anything to fill in the time and earn a few dollars. His luck turned when he was

called to the Woodstock Little Theatre to unplug a clogged lavatory bowl. While he was there an actor who was playing the part of a Texan swaggerer fell sick. There was no replacement to hand. The director's eyes fell on the glowering plumber with the snub nose and lantern jaw. At six feet two he sure looked like a tall Texan. . . .

That's how it all started. By the time the sick actor returned, Lee was a regular member of the troupe. Three years of summer stock and then Lee was on stage in New York, when he met Henry Hathaway, the film director, who was looking for extras for a Gary Cooper opus, *You're in the Navy Now* (1951). He was promised three days' work which extended to three weeks and then it was off with Hathaway to Hollywood, fame and fortune.

He played bit parts at first and the following year was going strong in heavy roles such as the leader of a lynch mob in *Duel at Silver Creek* (1952), an Audie Murphy oater.

He enjoyed himself immensely hurling boiling coffee into Gloria Grahame's face and stubbing his cigarette out on the back of Carolyn Jones' hand in *The Big Heat* (1953).

After such an appealing performance how could he fail to reach the heights of stardom?

His Westerns have been varied and many. In date order his best are *The Comancheros* (1961) and *The Man Who*

The spectacle of James Stewart, as an attorney-at-law, having to work as a waiter arouses the merriment of Lee Marvin as Liberty Valance and his two aides, Lee Van Cleef and Strother Martin. The film was The Man Who Shot Liberty Valance, *directed by John Ford (John Ford Production-Paramount).*

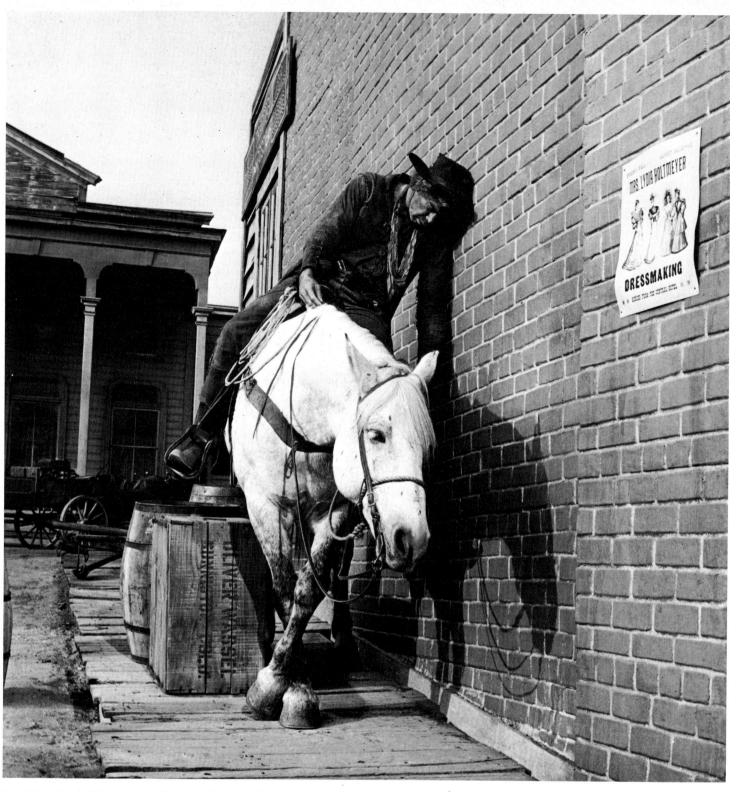

Lee Marvin as Kid Sheleen in Cat Ballou. *Lee played the dual role of Sheleen and his no-good silver-nosed brother Tim Strawn. The movie scored a tremendous hit in 1965 (Hecht Co.).*

Opposite: Paint Your Wagon. *The stars were Clint Eastwood, Lee Marvin and Jean Seberg (Alan J. Lerner 1969).*

Shot Liberty Valance (1962) both with John Wayne; *Cat Ballou* (1965) in which he played twins, one an amiable drunk, the other a sadistic killer with a silver nose; *The Professionals* (1966) with Burt Lancaster and Jack Palance; *Paint Your Wagon* (1969), a musical Western with Clint Eastwood (Lee's monosyllabic droning of 'I was born under a wandering star' was a top hit); and *Monte Walsh* (1970) in which he and Jack Palance were two forlorn cowboys riding through the sunset of the old West. The book was

written by Jack Shaeffer, author of *Shane*.

For his outstanding performance in *Cat Ballou* Lee won the Motion Picture Academy's Oscar for Best Actor of 1965. He has been married twice. In 1951 he married Betty Edeling and four children were born of the marriage. He and Betty were divorced in 1967 and in 1970 he married an old friend of his schooldays, Pamela Feeley.

Lee's star still shines brightly amongst the luminaries of Hollywood. May it shine for many years to come.

Infrequent but Welcome: Robert Duvall

Regrettably, Robert Duvall has not made many Westerns but although his appearances are infrequent they are very welcome to the discerning filmgoer.

One word aptly sums up the varying roles that he has played in all his films: immaculate. Watching him, one is aware that he has studied his part from every angle and in great depth and further, that he has considered the motivations of the role he is portraying to the extent that no matter how off-beat the character may be, his interpretation renders that character perfectly credible. Everything about him bespeaks his passion for exactness.

Robert Duvall was born, the son of a Rear Admiral, in San Diego, California, in 1931. Not for him a life on the ocean wave, though, and by the late 1950s he was performing in small theatres in New York. Friends noticed that he was always unobtrusively observing them, remarking their reactions and humours. So, too, did he constantly study the work of other actors, absorbing their characteristics. He was to plough all this concentration into his acting.

He reached stardom in *The Godfather* (1972) and even Marlon Brando in his Oscar-winning role as the Mafia boss, replete with stuffed cheeks, could not overshadow him as Tom O'Hagan, the legal adviser (consigliere) who takes on all the dirty jobs with a serene indifference.

His Westerns may be few but in all of them he has radiated immense power. In 1969 he played the scornful outlaw Ned Pepper, put paid to by John Wayne's Rooster Cogburn in *True Grit*. In *The Great Northfield Minnesota Raid* (1971) his Jesse James is far from the quasi-hero Tyrone Power made him back in 1939. He is grubby, unshaven, menacing and close to madness, a desperate man at war with the approaching tide of civilization in the form of baseball and railroads.

In *Lawman* (1971), Burt Lancaster as a crusading sheriff hunting down seven killers cannot stifle Duvall's compelling presence in the film. In villainy he is utterly ruthless. Could *anyone* be as totally and uncompromisingly ferocious as Duvall's cattleman in *Joe Kidd* (1972)? Duvall's performance answers 'yes'. Those cattle barons with their thousands of acres did wield their power mercilessly.

His most recent film with a Western setting is *Tender Mercies* (1983), an exceptional performance that brought him the accolade of an Oscar for best actor. Once again he plays a completely different part, that of Mac Sledge, a down-and-out singer of country-and-western ditties, fighting latent alcoholism in a struggle to win the lasting love of his new and second wife, Rosalie, played by Tess Harper.

In private life, Robert Duvall is a retiring man, his hobby being tennis and his recreation enjoying gourmet food.

Opposite and bottom: Robert Duvall illustrates the more sympathetic side of his acting in Tender Mercies *(EMI/Antron Media 1983).*

Below: Robert Duvall's Jesse James is a conscienceless mad-dog killer in The Great Northfield Minnesota Raid *in 1971 (Universal/ Robertson and Associates).*

Rock Star Cowboy: Kris Kristofferson

Opposite: We're back with the Younger Brothers, the James Brothers and the Ford Brothers yet again. The Carradine boys, David, Keith and Robert, are the Youngers. The movie was a 1980 success. Its title? The Long Riders *(Huka Films/United Artists).*

Below: Pat Garrett and Billy the Kid *which Sam Peckinpah directed in 1973 was that year's best Western. Billy is Kris Kristofferson, here seen on the left. James Coburn played the enigmatic Pat Garrett (MGM).*

Towards the end of the 1970s an attempt was made to bring about a revival in the fortunes of Western films. The effort did not succeed. *Buffalo Bill and the Indians*, a Paul Newman/Burt Lancaster epic, aroused little interest. Neither did Clint Eastwood's *Bronco Billy* (1980), nor Steve McQueen's *Tom Horn* (1980), good films though they were. Only *The Long Riders* (1980) with John Carradine's three sons, David, Keith and Robert, as the infamous Younger Brothers, really scored.

Thus, it was neither a favourable time for Westerns in general nor for United Artists to contemplate a filmic re-examination of the bloody Johnson County War which had taken place in Wyoming in 1892. Powerful cattlemen, furious with the inroads into their lands which were being carried out by home-steaders, small ranchers and rustlers, gathered together an army of hired gun-fighters to wipe out those pesky nuisances. The homesteaders and lowly ranchers struck back and troops of the 5th Cavalry had to be rushed in to save the hides of the gunslingers. Altogether it was a very messy business – and a ripe subject for a movie.

The not inconsiderable sum of five and three-quarter million dollars was allocated to the film and just to ensure its ultimate success a wonder-director was assigned. This was Michael Cimino whose Vietnam war film *The Deer Hunter* (1978) had won praise in all quarters and no less than five Academy Awards.

Kris Kristofferson was to head the cast. It was not Kris's first Western. He had appeared with James Coburn in *Pat*

Garrett and Billy the Kid (1973) which had been directed by that doyen of directors, Sam Peckinpah. For once, though, Sam had faltered. The film was boring and dull. It is possible that Kris was hoping for better luck with *The Johnson County War* as the new Western was then titled. If he did, then his hopes did not materialize.

Kris was born 22 June 1936, the son of an Air Force general, in Brownsville, Texas and raised in California. After graduation from Pomona College, he crossed the Atlantic to England and studied at Oxford as a Rhodes Scholar. When it came to military service, it seemed only natural that, the son of an Air Force officer, he would join the air arm. He served for five years, flying helicopters in Germany.

On his return to civilian life, he went to Nashville, Tennessee and worked in a recording studio. He started to compose and sing and by 1971 was well known as a rock star. Then he went to Hollywood where he debuted in *Cisco Pike* as a pop singer.

Now he was ready for *The Johnson County War*. However, from the moment Michael Cimino arrived by helicopter to inspect the Western township which had been erected for the film, costs began to escalate *fast*. For a start, the entire set was razed and reconstructed six feet further back from its original site. Cost of same? One million dollars.

Michael Cimino had started where he meant to continue. The total sum spent on the film when completed was forty million dollars. Did the United Artists' front room boys take heart when they reflected that with all that money the movie, now retitled *Heaven's Gate* (1980) was *bound* to be a success? If so, they were cruelly disappointed.

Its fate can perhaps be summed up by a comment from *Variety* which reported during the week of its first showing, 'It's been a bad week for show business – the MGM Grand Hotel fire in Las Vegas, the deaths of Mae West, George Raft and *Heaven's Gate.*'

To date, the film has not recovered from its lamentable première. It has been withdrawn, chopped about, shown again and withdrawn again. Currently there are two versions running to three hours and four hours respectively.

French film critics liked it. American critics didn't. Michael Cimino's direction has received a bad press. Were *The Deer Hunter* and his other winner, *Thunderbolt and Lightfoot* (1974) mere flashes in the pan? Does Cimino resemble Edgar Allen Poe who was once described as 'three fifths genius and two fifths sheer fudge?'

Heaven's Gate has done little to restore the flagging interest in Westerns. But maybe someday their popularity will return. Not for a long time, though, are any likely to cost 40 million dollars.

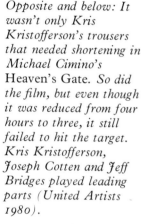

Opposite and below: It wasn't only Kris Kristofferson's trousers that needed shortening in Michael Cimino's Heaven's Gate. *So did the film, but even though it was reduced from four hours to three, it still failed to hit the target. Kris Kristofferson, Joseph Cotten and Jeff Bridges played leading parts (United Artists 1980).*

The Oscar Winners

In Old Arizona. 1928/29. Fox. Directors: Raoul Walsh, Irving Cummings. With Warner Baxter, Dorothy Burgess, Edmund Lowe. Oscar: Best Actor, Warner Baxter.

Cimarron. 1930. Paramount. Director: Wesley Ruggles. With Richard Dix, Irene Dunne. Oscars: Best Picture, William La Baron (producer); Best Writing Adaptation, Howard Estabrook; Best Art Director, Max Ree.

Stagecoach. 1939. United Artists. Director, John Ford. With John Wayne, George Bancroft, John Carradine, Andy Devine, Thomas Mitchell, Claire Trevor. Oscars: Best Supporting Actor, Thomas Mitchell; Best Music Score, Richard Hageman, Franke Harling, John Leipold and Leo Shuken.

The Westerner. 1940. Sam Goldwyn Production, released through United Artists. Director, William Wyler. With Gary Cooper, Walter Brennan, Doris Davenport. Oscar: Best Supporting Actor, Walter Brennan.

The Paleface. 1948. Paramount. Director, Norman Z. McLeod. With Bob Hope, Jane Russell, Robert Armstrong. Oscar: Best Song ('Buttons and Bows' by Jay Livingstone and Ray Evans).

She Wore a Yellow Ribbon. 1949. RKO. Director, John Ford. With John Wayne, Joanne Dru, Ben Johnson, Harry Carey Jr, Victor McLaglen. Oscar: Best Colour Cinematography, Winton C. Hoch.

High Noon. 1952. United Artists. Director, Fred Zinneman. With Gary Cooper, Lloyd Bridges, Grace Kelly, Thomas Mitchell. Oscars: Best Actor, Gary Cooper; Best Editing, Elmo Williams and Harry Gerstad; Best Music Score of a Drama or Comedy, Dimitri Tiomkin; Best Song ('High Noon', Dimitri Tiomkin, music, and Ned Washington, lyrics).

Calamity Jane. 1953. Warner Bros. Director, David Butler. With Doris Day, Howard Keel. Oscar, Best Song ('Secret Love' by Sammy Fain, music, and Paul Francis Webster, lyrics).

Shane. 1953. Paramount. Director, George Stevens. With Alan Ladd, Jean Arthur, Van Heflin, Brandon De Wilde. Oscar: Best Colour Cinematography, Loyal Griggs.

Oklahoma. 1955. Magna Picture, released by RKO. Director, Fred Zinneman. With Gordon Macrae, Shirley Jones, Gloria Grahame, Rod Steiger. Oscars: Best Scoring of a Musical, Robert Russell Bennett, Jay Blackton and Adolph Deutsch; Best Sound Recording, Fred Hynes.

The Big Country. 1958. United Artists. Director, William Wyler. With Gregory Peck, Jean Simmons, Burl Ives, Charles Bickford. Oscar: Best Supporting Actor, Burl Ives.

The Alamo. 1960. United Artists. Director, John Wayne. With John Wayne, Richard Widmark, Laurence Harvey, Richard Boone. Oscar: Best Sound, Gordon E. Sawyer and Fred Hynes.

Hud. 1963. Paramount. Director, Martin Ritt. With Paul Newman, Melvyn Douglas, Patricia Neal. Oscars: Best Actress, Patricia Neal; Best Supporting Actor, Melvyn Douglas; Best Black and White Cinematography, James Wong Howe.

How the West Was Won. 1963. MGM. Directors, John Ford, Henry Hathaway, George Marshall. With Gregory Peck, James Stewart, Henry Fonda, Richard Widmark, Debbie Reynolds, John Wayne. Oscars: Best Story and Screenplay, James R. Webb; Best Editing, Harold F. Kress; Best Sound, Franklin E. Milton.

Cat Ballou. 1965. Columbia. Director, Eliot Silverstein. With Jane Fonda, Lee Marvin. Oscar: Best Actor, Lee Marvin.

Butch Cassidy and the Sundance Kid. 1969. Twentieth Century-Fox. Director, George Roy Hill. With Paul Newman, Robert Redford, Katharine Ross. Oscars: Best Story and Screenplay, William Goldman; Best Cinematography, Conrad Hall; Best Original Music Score, Burt Bacharach; Best Song ('Raindrops keep falling on my head', Burt Bacharach, music, and Hal David, lyrics).

True Grit. 1969. Paramount. Director, Henry Hathaway. With John Wayne, Glen Campbell, Kim Darby. Oscar: Best Actor, John Wayne.

Tender Mercies. 1983. Antron Media for EMI. Director: Bruce Beresford. With Robert Duvall, Tess Harper, Allan Hubbard. Oscar: Best Actor, Robert Duvall.

Index